AID INDIA

A TWELVE YEAR HUMAN RIGHTS INVESTIGATION IN RURAL INDIA

Carole Stora-Calté

Ouka & Co

AID INDIA:

A TWELVE YEAR HUMAN RIGHTS INVESTIGATION IN RURAL INDIA

ISBN 978-2-9552150-5-0

published by Ouka & Co.

AID INDIA

A TWELVE YEAR HUMAN RIGHTS INVESTIGATION IN RURAL INDIA

"Poverty is the denial of all human rights….
Over a billion people around the world are deprived of their human dignity,
and the world is deprived of their creativity, ingenuity and productivity –
this should be enough cause for concern for anybody."

Professor Muhammad Yunus

Contents

Introduction

When I first decided to do that work, I knew that I wanted to do something on human rights and development issues. This is an investigation in rural India, which covers a twelve year period: from 2007 (when I went there for the first time) to 2019. I chose a non-governmental organization (NGO) that was leading effective actions both on human rights' violations and on development programs, especially one of them: microcredit.

AID India (Action in Disabilities India) is a non-profit organization (NPO), located in Tamilnadu, one of the twenty-nine states in India. Tamilnadu is also one of the poorest states and with a very high crime rate committed against women. In India and especially in rural areas, people of lower scheduled caste (the Dalits for example), especially women and disabled people, are in plight. The society despises them and consequently they live in extreme poverty and often suffer from nutritional deficiencies. They do not have access to education (most of them are illiterate), proper medical services and job opportunities. Due to a lack of education and awareness they do not realize the benefits of sending their children to school, and a lot of them have never been to a school. Since their earliest age, they go with their parents working on the fields or in private companies in awful conditions and for a miserable income. To add to their misfortune, the tsunami of 2004 completely devastated their lives, as most of them (even those who were not on the seashore) are involved more or less directly in the fishing industry. Although the international community, as we saw from our countries, mobilized, and that billions were sent to the affected countries (among which India, and especially Tamilnadu), just a few of the money reached them, as it was embezzled by the local organizations and authorities, not only governmental (to which AID India is used to face) but also ecclesiastical since the Roman Catholic Church (considered as a minority in India and thus beneficiating of the minority privilege) is very powerful in the area. It is through this experience that I was able to see with my own eyes, and analyze, how the NGO, in view of the local constraints, as regards of political and legal matters and especially in terms of violations of human rights[1], can overcome the difficulties in its mission of economic and social development, based in particular on the Grameen Bank's system as founded by Prof. M. Yunus.

The Grameen Bank's system, based on microcredit, was created by Prof. M. Yunus while there was a devastating famine in Bangladesh. Seeing that it was not a shortage of food (thanks to the technological and agricultural innovations), but the lack of money to buy it, that made people starving, he went out from the academic life and decided to do something about hunger. Hunger was for him a significant symptom of poverty, underlining that economic development's processes only beneficiate to a very few people and countries. The reason of this, as a matter of fact, is credit. As Prof. M. Yunus says "Money is power"[2]. The most critical problem for most of the people is the difficulty they have to access loans, whereas the only way to help them to get out of poverty would be precisely to allow them access to credit while ensuring loans repayment. As an economist, Prof. M. Yunus knew that the financial help from developed countries was not a long-term solution to overcome poverty, regarding the old saying "give a man a fish, feed him for a day, teach a man how to fish, and you feed him for life". The best way to overcome poverty was of course to help people starting their own business. Nevertheless, banks were extremely reluctant to give loans

---

[1] Cf. PART I "The problem of corruption in the tsunami-affected area"
[2] YUNUS Muhammad, *Acceptance speech at the award ceremony of the World Food Price*, December 1994.

to poor people since they were wondering, because of an old cliché, if they were "creditworthy" and did not want to take any risks of non-repayment. However, Prof. M. Yunus decided to develop it himself, borrowing at the beginning with his own resources, and focusing especially on women, who are the most disadvantaged in many societies (Bangladesh, India and so on).

After seeing his double success (that is to say almost a one hundred percent rate of repayment for banks and a community more respectful towards women for development programs), banks and institutions started to give funds more easily. As a matter of fact, they were even very interested, because they didn't only have a perfect repayment, but they even made benefits out of it. It is in this context that AID India's general secretary, Mr. S. Peter Raj, decided in 2000 to start his own microcredit program[3], after getting training directly with its founder Prof. M. Yunus in Bangladesh. The microcredit program is a continuous and growing success in Tamilnadu.

As I will explain here, human rights and development are big issues, but the fundraising process, that is to say soliciting and gathering money for the projects, is an even more difficult work since the embezzlement of funds is a well-known phenomenon. On that topic, AID India is closely related to AVE MARIA, the other NGO Mr. S. Peter Raj is involved in. I spent a lot of time studying the subject of human rights' violations in the area, to understand fully the disastrous consequences of the embezzlements (since the money dedicated to the poor doesn't reach them). Thus, I started to gather all the elements concerning the embezzlement of the tsunami funds, and the other frauds that take place in the region (committed either from priests, government officials or NGOs). I also transcribed important documents to be published on the website (a priest's letter addressed to the Vatican, a complaint from the fishermen group) and realized reports of meetings which were lead in order to organize future actions, like demonstrations to attract the government's attention, and with

---

[3] Cf. PART II "The microcredit program's effectiveness and the Self-Help Groups"

the avowed aim of attracting even more influential associations or institutions working on human rights' issues.

That is why, in the first part of this work, I will present the problems related to the various violations of human rights, context in which the NGO has to progress and fight, in order to be able to make its different development programs more effective.

In the second part, I will present the microcredit program which was set up by the NGO and show the great impact it has, that is to say the way it works, and why it is definitely one of the best ways for the people to get out of misery.

PART I The current situation: major issues and potential solutions

Corruption is one of the major problems in India. One can measure how much it affects all kinds of projects we want to realize. Indeed, this is a very concerning issue because it reaches all layers of society, and in the case of Tamilnadu also the clergy. In 2007, the main issue I worked on was the embezzlement of the tsunami funds. Tamilnadu State, as one of the areas which was the most severely affected by the tsunami in December 2004, received financial help from the tremendous collection of money that took place in North America and Europe in particular. But, while I was gathering all the elements concerning the embezzlement of the tsunami funds, it was obvious that most of this was committed, not only by some government officials but also by priests.

This also led me to participate in meetings for the organization of demonstrations to attract the government's attention, so that they take proper actions against them (at least withdrew some of their privileges, like the title of "official correspondent", which would weaken them). For this, I also made the report of different meetings, and especially two of them, one with the fishermen group and another with some other like-minded teams, because many of them were much more informal, as it is usual here, around a cup of tea. Therefore, I didn't take notes about all of them, either for groups or individuals, like the many teachers who were victims of frauds in different Catholic schools in the area.

I also transcribed important documents to be published on the website, such as a priest's letter addressed to the Vatican, which is extremely rare as they have to obey to the hierarchy law, and a complaint of the fishermen group.

In all cases, it was extremely interesting to see all the violations of human rights in the area, not only to establish reports and gather proofs but also in order to see how and what the NGOs (AVE MARIA in close collaboration with AID India) had to face, trying to adapt and handle (and of course why the work of the two NGOs can't be separated from each other).

I. The problem of corruption

After a few meetings I found out how much corruption is devastating the country, and Tamilnadu is not an exception. On the one hand, there was the powerful Roman Catholic Church with a very high number of corrupted priests under the guidance of the local bishop, and on the other hand (which is more known but not less problematic) different NGOs and government officials involved in many kinds of frauds. But in all this, the most critical was the phenomenon's extent, which is getting bigger as nothing is done against it.

A) The bishop and priests' embezzlements in Tamilnadu

Tuticorin is a city in Tamilnadu in South India, which is also the headquarters of the Tuticorin Roman Catholic Diocese, with bishop Yvon Ambroise at the head. This diocese is running many Catholic schools, using minority right (privilege given by the Indian government to establish schools easily, since the Christians are meager in number in Indian population) which is conferred by the Indian constitution to give educational benefit to religious minorities.

1. *AVE MARIA's creation and its fights*

The problem is that the local bishop, namely bishop Yvon Ambroise[4], making use of this privilege, crushes the employees of the schools by means of compulsory donations, transfers, suspensions, dismissals, illegal deductions etc. He and many of the priests under his diocese have gone to the extent of doing many kinds of frauds using the money earned from the teachers and poor children. He involves in all kinds of illegalities, directly and indirectly, through his agents who are available in the name of superintendent of RC Schools and correspondents (priests) at the grassroots levels.

Peter Raj, AID India's general secretary, started in 1998 an association namely "Association of Veteran Employees of Minority Academic Recognized Institutions of All kind" (AVE MARIA), to fight against the illegalities of this diocese. But its representations remained fruitless, even after approaching the government officers, as they do not involve, either because they are afraid of the priests who are quite powerful, or because they are bought, since corruption is a major issue in the area. Thus, the association went to the court and got an order for stopping illegal deductions. But they still do not stop and they do not obey the orders of the court. AVE MARIA's general secretary, along with its partners from SOS Diritti Umani in Italy, distributed flyers at the Vatican in Rome, but even after sending a number of petitions to the Vatican and to the higher authorities, nothing changed.

In order to impress and intimidate the people, the priests in Tamilnadu started to punish the active people who work against their illegalities by means of suspension and dismissal from their jobs. Therefore AVE MARIA joined hands with Humanist Movement International. On July 4th, 2007, from Roma, SOS Diritti Umani and AVE MARIA sent a petition to the right person to take action against this bishop. But there was no use: they directed a cardinal in India to take action. But nothing happened since the one responsible of the

---

[4] On January, 17, 2019 he retired. A new bishop, Antony Pillai Stephen, was announced by the Vatican. He has taken charge on February, 24, 2019. Obviously, situation has improved.

Catholic Church in India is precisely the one who appointed this bishop in Tamilnadu, as they know each other very well. In the meantime, on September 11, 2007, there was a big commotion in front of the bishop's house in Tuticorin, demanding the accounts for the tsunami funds which the bishop misused instead of giving it back to the people. As he did not do anything about this, AVE MARIA created a website[5] in order to publish everything with all proofs. Again nothing changed, since the group under bishop Yvon Ambroise is very powerful, and cannot be controlled by anyone either in India or anywhere else, except by the Roman Catholic Church itself (which started to have more supervision a few years ago, but obviously not very successfully).

2. The illegalities and their consequences

a. Misappropriation of funds

The most affected are the poor children, who are studying in their institutions. They demand a lot of money as fees from the poor children. Most of the children cannot pay this money. Consequently, they become dropouts and child laborers. Since most of the parents are illiterates and poor, they cannot fight against this rock of money. And since the bishop and priests have a lot of money they easily buy all persons and the law too. As a matter of fact now, the whole community here is spoilt by their illegalities. The most paradoxical in this situation is that bishop Yvon Ambroise was also the chairman of the Peace and Justice Committee and was the president of many financial committees worldwide in many funding agencies, since, as he used to work in Caritas India, he also had the confidence of all other NGOs etc. But no one knew what he was doing with the money he was receiving. As we can see in AVE MARIA's website, the

---

[5] Cf. AVE MARIA's website on www.catholicschoolsatrocities.org

bishop has never given transparent account to the fishermen community with regard to the tsunami fund he got from international organizations[6].

Hence, not only affected from the tsunami disaster (that is fortunately now a remote memory), corruption is the second calamity the people in Tamilnadu had to fight against. And even with many kinds of information and proofs, and decisions from the Tamilnadu's supreme court, there were still major violations of human rights in this area.

b. Cases of sexual harassment and drinking

Indeed, there is also a number of cases of sexual harassment. But, even if it is proved, it is totally concealed by the bishop. Such priests would be sent to foreign countries for some years and when they come back, the crime is already forgotten or some new problems are being dealt with. Since the people are God-fearing, they do not want to go against the bishop and priests. There is a superstition that if someone goes against a bishop or priest, the whole family will be destroyed by God. This is what they always tell at the altar when they celebrate mass.

c. Briberies in the school administration, towards the children and teachers

The main problem, concerning the corrupted priests in the area, is the many ways of misusing funds. Indeed, if there has been a major problem with regard to the tsunami fund the bishop got from international organizations (not being able to give transparent account to the fishermen community who was asking for that), there is still a big issue concerning the briberies in the school administration[7].

Illegalities against the children

When there are many eligible candidates in schools for promotion of headmistress posts, they bring other people from other districts freely without con-

---

[6] However, after some time, his FCRA account through which he was getting funds from abroad was cancelled by central government.

[7] Unfortunately, briberies have been going on for years and never stopped.

sidering the legal and individual rights of the teachers working in the school. There is no seniority list in the schools. The court's orders are not respected by the department either. And they also go hand in hand because they get a lot of money from the management. As an example, the headmistress (who is a nun) of St. Joseph's Girls Higher Secondary School, Satankulam, Tuticorin district, Tamilnadu, South India, namely Mercy Anthony Gerard has been brought from another district and another management illegally, and in spite of several representations she got approval and salary from the department. It is against the existing rules. But if AVE MARIA wants to go to the court to protest, it also needs money for that, which is not always easy. So it cannot fight until the last. Making use of this weakness, they keep on doing all these illegalities. It was also found that this headmistress also collects a lot of money from the children for being late and uses the money for her own purpose[8]. Actually, the school must start at 9:30 a.m. in the morning, but she asks the students to come by 9 a.m. Since the children cannot reach school by nine because of the distance from their house, she collects money. Another example was given when the orphans of She Home (orphanage run by AID India) were asked for money by the nun (manager of the school), for being three minutes late. She was refusing their inscription until AVE MARIA called her (since she knows she was risking to be brought to the court, she stopped).

But in order to have the law respected, the association always needs to take action, meet people and collect proofs. In the school, the children are getting corporal punishments too, which is common, in particular in the Roman Catholic School at Virudhunagar near AID India's orphanage "Island of Hope". In this school too, the headmistress is a nun. But even if AVE MARIA makes complaints before her, she does not care about it and the assistant teachers are still violent in the classrooms. Big representations were made, and after that it has more or less come down. But they collect lot of fees from the disadvantaged children, against the government rules. If the children do not pay it, they avenge

[8] Now she has retired but the successor does the same.

on them for not giving them the money. And since the parents are poor and illiterates they cannot raise voice against the atrocities and illegalities.

Illegalities against the teachers

There were also illegalities, not only against the children, but also committed against the teachers themselves. The school management almost always gets bribery for making appointments in the schools run by them. They make illegal deductions in the name of their service charge, which is illegal[9]. For example, a teacher is entitled to get salary of ten thousand rupees. The government gives the salary through the management. The management getsone thousand rupees and gives nine thousand rupees to the teacher. But the teacher has to sign the salary register for having received ten thousand rupees because they do keep records and signature from the employees as if the employees get the entire salary. Hence it is not a problem for the management during audit time. If someone raises voice against this, immediately they are punished. This money is spent by the bishop for his own purpose, and for going against the teachers in the supreme court.

Of course, there are many other ways they used to get money, either from the people and their children, the teachers, or the government. Another fraud was the misrepresentation a priest made, in order to get support from the government and appoint one of his relatives as a teacher. As a matter of fact, fifty children are needed to ask for financial help and be able to appoint a new teacher. But the number of students was not sufficient in that school. So the priest decided to "borrow" fifteen children from another Catholic school with false documents (which constitutes an offence for forgery and use of forged documents)[10].

Unfortunately, the priests are not the only ones to make abuses and misuses, NGOs and government officials are also very often involved.

---

[9] Unfortunately, these practices (asking money from children, making illegal deduction) did not stop. It is still going on, now in 2019.
[10] They still make false documents to appoint a new teacher and get the money out of it in 2019.

B) The corrupted NGOs and government officials

If we still consider corruption, and go out of the religious side, the picture is not rosy either. As one often hears, many NGOs are not as much dedicated to the cause as they claim - even worse, they are "phantom NGOs" just created to get funds, which bring the other "clean" NGOs in a very delicate situation. It is in fact harder and harder to get funds when no funding agencies trust them anymore. But which make things even more complicated is the implication of some government officials: when they are supposed to denounce the fake NGOs or the ones abusing their status, they too often support the ones who give them bribery.

1. Phantom NGOs and "profit" NPOs

The work realized by the NGOs may be one of the best ways to empower the people and help them to get out from poverty, however, any statement has to be done with an extreme caution. As a matter of fact, if some NGOs such as AID India are totally dedicated to their work, some of them are totally fake. There would be thousands of fake NGOs only in Madras, Tamilnadu, India. Indeed, this is a great problem for the funding agencies, banks, or firms, which are more and more reluctant to allocate credits to the many NGOs which are asking them. Some of the NGOs are only aimed to receive the money, and soon vanish into thin air. Others, more common than the fake NGOs, are settled for a while to prosper out of the funds they receive, giving just a part of it to the people to whom it is addressed to. As a responsible of a Cambodian NGO, which Mr S. Peter Raj knew, said: "Why are you giving all that, I'm giving the people about twenty-five percent of what I get, and I'm still one of the NGOs which give the most". These fake NGOs and NGOs, whose purpose is to make profit (but which fortunately started to be blacklisted by the government aware of that), still cause a great issue of credibility for the other NGOs like AID India, which are doing well and even are losing money when they have to handle such a terrible event like the tsunami in order to meet the people's most basic and urgent needs.

Indeed, the after-tsunami is one of the matters the NGO had to deal with for several years, not only because of the priests and local authorities' embezzlement but also because, out of urgency, AID India sent all the necessary and in the meantime had to forget the loans already given and which will never be reimbursed. Moreover, the NGO had to repay it itself, at the same time it was trying to help the people to survive, knowing that for a long-term assistance they will need a new loan to start another business again. That is, actually, what happened in the many coastal villages AID India was working in, and that I visited in order to assess the needs and see the possibilities of giving new loans or, even better, grants. Therefore, while some NGOs were misappropriating the money, others like AID India had to face a big loss. On March 31st 2007, the amount of outstanding loan, that is to say the credit they still have with them, was Rs 6,658,208. This should have been less than the amount of loan given, which was for the same period Rs 5,850,000. But, since the NGO was repaying the loans of the beneficiaries, who lost everything with the tsunami and were not able to do so, and at the same time providing them basic needs and new loans, the amount of outstanding loan increased dramatically. This constitutes an example of AID India's transparency and is one of the reasons why all board members are volunteers (so that they are not members to receive money but to contribute to the NGO's prosperity and the one of the beneficiaries).

But, to make sure that the funds are not misused when it is sent by the government monitors have to come to the NGOs and make all the necessary checking before validating the demand - monitors who are also, often, corrupted.

2. The interest of the government officials

In order to see the utilization of funds by the NGOs, when they get loans from the central government, monitors are sent. In that way, they can see, if all the funds have been given as loans properly for creating assets and for starting businesses. But the monitors are also corrupted. As an example, AID India had to fill a form for one of its projects, the monitor came and noticed everything was perfectly run and in order. But to validate the demand, the monitor asked for bribery and as the NGO refused, said firmly that if other NGOs do, AID India will also have to do so. But the NGO held out and made a complaint before the government, arguing that, if necessary, they will go to the court showing the document signed by the monitor stipulating that everything was fine.

T.T. Krishnan, the monitor, was finally transferred from Delhi to Bombay, and the form was validated. But a few months later, for a similar demand, the NGO was again confronted to the same man, because in the various administrative offices, this one had been chosen to come for the supervision and T.T. Krishnan had not been dismissed. Again the NGO had to make a complaint because again this man asked for money. Now, in 2020, this problem is solved.

Sir Chandrika Prasad Srivastava, Indian diplomat, who was for sixteen years secretary general of the International Maritime Organization, and received a knighthood after his retirement, on the recommendation of the British government, as Knight Commander in the Most Distinguished Order of St. Michael and St. George, is recognized for his work in the United Nations and his integrity. According to him, corruption is a threat to the country's welfare as "the economic development of the country is severely handicapped by an inadequate, inefficient and ill-maintained infrastructure whose functioning is hampered by indescribable malpractices"[11]. He clearly shows that only when corruption is eradicated, especially at the top level, it is then possible to take charge of the overwhelming poverty which still affects 364 million Indians according to the

---

[11] SRIVASTAVA Chandrika Prasad, *Corruption – India's enemy within*, New Delhi: Macmillan India, 2001, 240p

2018 multidimensional poverty index (MPI)[12]. As a matter of fact, corruption is "on the rampage, depriving the people of fair administration and thwarting the process of development". And to add: "public funds allocated for the welfare of the desperately poor are largely siphoned off into private pockets". Only the ones who have the resources can have what they want, and despite the recent anti corruption campaigns, these practices are largely accepted. Besides that, the caste system is extremely rigid, which make things even more difficult for the people if they want to change it, each one having a certain place assigned. To the four main castes (the *brahmans* at the top traditionally in charge of the rituals and Holy Texts' knowledge, the *kshatriya* holding the temporal power, the *vaishya* for the production and trade markets and the *shudra* for all service functions), we can add the ones who are outside the system of castes and referred as *parias* (considered as untouchable because touching them would cause a ritual impurity). Even though it was abolished in 1947, this is only official because it is still alive in the Indian society today. This system is even more complicated as the main castes are themselves divided in thousands of sub-castes, so that it is very difficult to move from a caste to another, even if in some cases we can see that "caste no bar" (no barrier). But it remains very rare anyways, and most of all, outside the social conventions which let the parents choose for their child a husband or wife, usually from the same background (partly because it will be impossible for the bride's parents to pay the appropriate dowry, if the families are from two different castes).

In all cases, even if India is a democratic country, conservatism (and in particular casteism) is still very strong, strengthened by centuries of traditions. And the people seem resigned to corruption as something unfair but unavoidable, in such an extent that corruption spreads in all layers of society, given that low wages (and in particular in the administration) make them consider bribery as

---

[12] The 2018 global multidimensional poverty index (MPI) is released by the United Nations Development Program (UNDP) and the Oxford Poverty and Human Development Initiative (OPHI).

the only way for a decent living for them and their (usually big) family. The 2017 Corruption Perception Index[13] shows India as the eighty-first most corrupted country in the world, with a score of forty out of one hundred as more corrupted, falling two places compared to last year (score remaining the same which indicates that other countries improved, unlike India). Therefore, India is in a very critical situation because unless corruption is eliminated from the country, it will be almost impossible to "raise the standards of efficiency in administration as well as in the production and distribution of the necessary goods of life"[14]. This was the conclusion I came up to, and towards which the NGO had and will have to fight continuously. And this is why, to face all these difficulties, that many meetings were organized, either formal or (for most of them) informal, in the office or outside.

II. The reaction of the people and the NGO's role

Seeing all kinds of illegalities, the people in the area started to realize that something had to be done. Indeed, this took a certain time as they are all frequent churchgoers, and had a tough time to realize that, despite their oath, not all priests were following it. Therefore, and even if a large number of the population is still in an acceptance's position, many of them started to gather in order to change things. I have to specify that they were even more virulent because they didn't want that these priests tarnish their church's image. Most of them came because they trusted AVE MARIA and AID India, some of them knowing that AID India's president was a priest of an absolute integrity, and

[13] https://www.transparency.org/news/feature/corruption_perceptions_index_2017
[14] SRIVASTAVA Chandrika Prasad, *Corruption – India's enemy within*, New Delhi: Macmillan India, 2001, 240p

that the NGO won many cases before the Tamil supreme court, although that was not easy.

A) The fishermen community, and different like-minded teams

In Tamilnadu, unlike India, the Catholic community is not really a minority. The fishermen, along with the other teams I met, belong to that community and are strong believers and churchgoers. This is only after many frauds committed by some priests they realized something should be done in order that their faith would not be discredited.

1. Meeting with the fishermen group

I met the fishermen group. It was then obvious how important the problems were. There are two major points we can underline, concerning the problems in Tamilnadu state: first the school administration, and second the tsunami funds misused.

Education is a basic right of the children, which is not fully respected here. The money which should be spent for schools was kept until now by bishop Yvon Ambroise, with the assistance of a chancellor (Fr. Sathyanesan) and a superintendent (Father Kumar Raja) of Roman Catholic Schools. Persons changed but practice did not.

The same situation is observed concerning tsunami victims, who should have received financial support from the government, NGOs and international organizations. But just a few of the money was spent for them, as bishop Yvon Ambroise embezzled it.

A few years before that, there was no checking for the money given to the Roman Catholic Church, which is empowered with money in the state of Tamilnadu. But since some cases arrived to the court, demands of transparent accounts from the Catholic Church existed. Nevertheless, there is still no checking from the Indian or Tamilnadu's governments, neither from the different NGOs or international organizations providing money (even now in 2019). The main point is, as I said above, bishop Yvon Ambroise got the confidence of many organizations, since he was working in one of them (Caritas India) before being ordered bishop.

The three rules to become a priest (chastity, poverty and obedience) are obviously not followed, and it is proved that this man is totally corrupted. The fishermen group provided me with many examples of it, which are unfortunately still relevant today.

• First of all, it is proved that bishop gives empty paper with his signature so that the priest in power is able to use it in many ways, with the bishop's consent while he is travelling (and thus never available). These papers are used most of times to harass people (especially the needy and poor ones). This is still happening in 2020.

• A priest also sent a fake report about a village supposed to be on the seashore, and affected by the tsunami. In that way, he received money from Germany and kept it for himself. Priests still do keep money for themselves even when help is coming to support local communities.

• There are also cases of priests hiding their identity by not wearing the formal dress, in order to abuse people more easily (still a current practice).

• Even more striking, the fishermen organization built with its own money a school and houses for people, but the bishop took control over it, which causes two major problems: first, the fishermen are not even able to rule their own buildings and school, and second, the children cannot get admission in the school. Likewise, the teachers of the community cannot get employment opportunity in it. Establishing schools, indeed, is just like a business in this diocese. The employees are harassed by many illegalities of the management, which was headed by bishop Yvon Ambroise. These issues, to date, were not solved at all.

There are many irregularities which were taken to the judicial court, which recognized the illegalities. But even the judicial system failed as nothing was done and changed after the decision. When a priest is found to be guilty for a crime, he is sent abroad by the Catholic Church, and comes back when the controversy is over. He doesn't even get in trouble with the police as nobody tells it. Even the government approved people's actions against the Catholic Church's oppression, but a document was found showing that the bishop is not paying any attention to the government's decisions.

Therefore AVE MARIA, in collaboration with AID India, decided to publish a magazine called *Energy*, to make aware the people of Tamilnadu. After that, the Catholic Church asked to stop the publication, arguing they will give money for that. AVE MARIA refused: the church for some time tried to make pressure. It now stopped.

This led the fishermen community to the conclusion that the bishop and all corrupted priests in Tamilnadu had to be physically removed, and proper actions had to be taken. Then, they planned to go on hunger strike to demonstrate against the bishop, but they had to wait that he comes back from the Vatican, where he was trying to get some support.

2. Meeting with Edward George and Jeyasingh

This is an important fact to say that all kind of people in Tamilnadu were gathering to strike against injustice. On Nov 27th, 2007, two men, namely Edward George and Jeyasingh, came after reading AVE MARIA's magazine *Energy*. They felt attracted by it, as the magazine is dealing with all Human Rights' issues, especially the Roman Catholic Church's illegalities.

Edward George and Jeyasingh are businessmen working together with around two hundred other people on that issue, as a like-minded team, about all kind of social matters.

They collected information on many illegalities committed by priests in Tuticorin District (which was under bishop Yvon Ambroise's rule, and consisted in three different districts in Tamilnadu state, namely Tuticorin, Kanyakumari, and Tirunelveli). They came especially from Thisayanvilai village (which comes under Tirunelveli district) to Satankulam (which is in Thoothukudi district) in order to meet AID India and AVEMARIA organizations.

The main issue that was talked about was all the problems caused by a single priest called Peter in their area. This priest is found to be corrupted and unethical.

Priest Peter came a few years before that, from another parish in a village called Anaikarai. Over there, he collected money illegally, out of the donations offered by the pilgrims who are coming to the village for this church. But since he was not satisfied enough with the interests he was getting with this money in the bank, he decided to make loans to people who would need it, with high interest rates. In that way, he became a sort of private money lender (the kind of persons AID India is fighting against in its microcredit program so that the people can get loans and avoid the money lenders with their high interest rates, which usually puts them into debt). But since it was not enough, also with that money and since he couldn't buy anything with his own name, he decided to buy many different assets (such as houses) on behalf of other people. Most of these people were found to be some of the many different mistresses he had, even if a Catholic priest is not supposed to.

As a matter of fact, one of his mistresses was a married woman called Nirmala Rani. And she was at the priest's house when her husband was murdered. The priest is suspected to have ordered this. Many times, Edward George and Jeyasingh tried to catch him red-handed overnight, but each time he managed to escape, as he built a special passage for this use only. It is also proved that the priest, who was not satisfied with the many girls he had, decided to run out with a nun.

He is also violent in his attitude and words, and another priest (namely Antonydoss) even beat Edward George as he was making reproaches to him. After that, the case was taken to the police, but even if he was defended by the police since they know him to be an immoral person, absolutely nothing changed and the priest is still threatening people.

Besides that, priest Peter was (and is still) demanding bribery for medical leaves and appointments from the 125 teachers, who were working in ten different schools, where the priest was the official correspondent (under bishop Yvon Ambroise's management) for the government. Of course, the teachers he is friend with are not required to, and even more: they are not required to come to the schools, but still get salary etc.As a matter of fact, the Tamil government would be able to take appropriate action, and at least withdraw his title of "official correspondent", which would weaken him. But no action is taken against him. Consequently, Edward George and Jeyasingh (with their whole team) decided to inform the right department through the sending of many letters and taking the case to the court. After that, nothing changed. So they went to bishop Yvon Ambroise and scolded him for not doing anything, but he did not even reply. In the end, the bishop never moved at all.

Moreover, these priests are also leading a divide-and-rule policy in the different villages, so that they can rule more easily. And these divisions, as Edward George and Jeyasingh said, are now like a disaster in the area. It was finally concluded that if one priest commits mistakes, immediate action should be taken, otherwise the problem becomes bigger. And even if he is transferred to another parish, the problem will not be solved but only transferred.

Therefore, after attending this meeting, they decided to join forces to go on a hunger strike to attract the attention of the government.

In that way, the NGO decided to call the fishermen group, which is also fighting for that, in order to go to Tuticorin to meet them and get permission from the police department for the demonstration. Unfortunately, when the bishop was coming back and the team was starting to distribute flyers to inform the people of the demonstration, the team was arrested for false allegations (even if they had proofs[15]) and stayed many days imprisoned, which postponed the hunger strike until it was possible for them to gather again. The results, even after they went on hunger strike, were still limited.

B) The NGO's important role

If AVE MARIA was created in order to come to the people's assistance because of the priests' illegalities (which make the living of the poor even harder), S. Peter Raj, one of its initiators, was already involved (and still is) in an NGO, which was aimed to deal with all the problems they faced in their day-to-day lives. Thus, the two are working closely together. AID India (Action In Disabilities India), which was established in the year 1992 as a registered NGO, was first focused in the welfare of people with disabilities in rural areas. As the organization became increasingly aware of the many needs of the communities, it enlarged its objectives to include the support of rural women, children, and people with special needs. The NGO accomplished this by enabling programs centered around health, education, awareness, and the promotion of the socio-economic development of these groups.

1. The organization

Since its foundation AID India has been working for the upliftment and the welfare of the poorest of the poor, and their reintegration in the society. It operates in rural areas, irrespective of caste, creed, sex and religion. Thus, it aims to develop these poor areas of India and to build a just, humane, self-reliant and sustainable society.

AID India used to have seven board members, they are six now (after the death of one of them). The president of this organization is Mr. A. Peter Rajah and the general secretary is Mr. S. Peter Raj. The other five members are women.

---

15 Cf. on AVE MARIA's website, for all proofs and further details on the actions taken

One among the five is a retired teacher and the remaining four are still working as teachers. Board members must have an interest in voluntary social work. This board meets every two months to evaluate and discuss existing programs and plans for the future. Directly under the president is the general secretary, who organizes and executes the programs with the help of his employees. All board members (including the president and general secretary) are volunteers. Apart from the board members, there are ten other people in the advisory board. They are teachers, professors, doctors etc. They mingle with the board every six months for making the programs useful to the beneficiaries.

Grama Vasantham program was created in April 2000. It was aiming at the eradication of poverty, and wanted to give self-confidence and force to low-caste women and people with disabilities.

This program was headed by AID India's general secretary, Mr. Peter Raj, and Miss Vimala, a disabled lady, who was the deputy manager. Two persons (Mr. Iyyappan and Mrs. Dency) were responsible of these activities on the field and also the staff's coordination. Finally, eleven other members were working in the program, they led monthly meetings and took care of the administrative tasks. Therefore, fifteen people were working in Grama Vasantham program. All of them were from Satankulam and around, so they knew the economic and social situation of the area, and the problems that the local population meets. In that way, the field workers were very close to the clients (the other name given to the beneficiaries) and able to get their confidence very easily. The female clients, often shy because of their social statute, usually express themselves more easily with people they know and trust. Besides, the staff could have the possibility to make them understand better some specific problems, such as health, social or education matters etc.

In order to work on the field, the staff had at least three years of experience in a charitable organization. All staff members attended training at least six-times a year about microfinance in general, about the novelties in that field, or the development's possibilities. Moreover, these trainings were an occasion for them to understand the others better, and more particularly the situation of the poorest, in order to help them in a more efficient way.

This microcredit program was such a success that the government has undertaken it. Loans are now given by the commercial bank. In 2020, AID India's role is to recommend the groups for loans. Many groups have become independent. They do not need more people for this program.

2. The activities undertaken

a. Health Program

Every year in summer a team of medical students from Creighton University (USA)[16] were coming to AID India to conduct free medical camps and to give awareness on general health care. They were giving medicines and small medical supplies to the dispensary and also conducted medical camps. With donations, the NGO was able to run this project. Eye camps, medical camps, general health programs and polio awareness programs were conducted freely. In 2017, already 2326 people had benefitted from these programs directly.

I had myself the opportunity to participate to a one day medical camp with the presence of doctors who came especially for this, and during which I assisted to their guidance and treatment, with distribution of medicines. Most of the people who came there were the beneficiaries of the microcredit program, because they were aware of the event thanks to the staff, even if leaflets and signs had been informing them in different villages (despite the fact more than sixty percent of the population don't know how to read and write, which is another priority for the NGO). Most of the people were mainly suffering from malnutrition (in seventy percent of the cases), and this is precisely why the microcredit program is so useful (because with self-employment they can afford a more decent living). As a matter of fact, as I noticed in the villages, many people eat

---

[16] Other groups also came. Now they have stopped coming from the US.

either rice or only fish (as many of them are involved in the fishing industry). The NGO's health worker goes in the villages especially to give them some vitamins, but they have many kinds of deficiencies, especially women, who are since their childhood less fed than the boys, which causes a major problem for the baby's development when they are pregnant. They do have many different types of food and a variety of vegetables and fruits, but those are mainly intended to export.

A pharmacy is also functioning and there is a health worker who goes in the villages with medicines for minor problems. When I came with this health worker into the villages in order to assist her, I assisted one time to the direct fight of a couple. I was following a traditional meeting with a group of people with disabilities when I heard a woman shouting and then crying. She went out: she had been beaten with a stick and had a big bump on her arm. Many people were present, especially women. She was moaning on the ground just next to me. Some people were talking to the man still yelling in the house. The staff (the nurse and another staff member who were with me) explained the situation to me: her husband was drunk and since he was having an affair with another woman, he was suspecting her to do the same each time she was out of the house. The woman was still crying, when the other women around told her (in Tamil, the staff translated for me) that she will have to keep quiet when her husband will say something and they will defend her. I don't know what that meant exactly, but mainly, as divorce is not accepted, the people have to live together whatever happens. She had two children and no other choice. The health worker made an injection and gave her some medicine, but of course it will not change her situation. This is a typical case of what is happening in the day-to-day life of the people in Tamilnadu.

b. Distance Child Adoption Program

Thanks to SOS Diritti Umani (Italy), in 2007 the NGO had adopted 192 children in the four districts. Since then, many children have completed studies and become independent. By the end of 2019, sixty-eight children are still supported. The children are supported in their educational needs. Also the community in which the children live are benefiting from this program by means of independent living through sustainable businesses. Child development centers and special tuition for the children are some of the programs to lift the children. Finding new sponsors reveals to be very difficult. Indeed, the people either are not interested or already involved in other programs, and the specialized NGOs (World Vision, Aide et Action etc.) already have contacts and don't want others, despite the reliability of this NGO.

c. Island of Hope – Orphanage in Virudhunagar

Initiated by Narovinu, Czech Republic, this orphanage is being run by AID India in Virudhunagar, with 102 children. This is supported by Narovinu as well as SOS Diritti Umani. In 2007, Sunflower Children (USA) were also helping. In the year 2007 only, the third floor construction was finished and it is used as a study hall and library for the children. The aim of this orphanage is to bring up the children in a humanist way. As I noticed during the time I spent there, the all round personality of the children is the focus of the orphanage. Children are living in a homely situation, and talk about the tutors and the director, respectively as their "family" and "father". Indeed, they forget their dramatic stories and often stop to be ashamed of their caste, when their friends in the school come with their parents in the orphanage. To them, as an example, having beds and tables are an outside sign of wealth which make them feel more comfortable and confident.

d. School: Sarva Sikshya Abiyan (SSA) and Maria Grace Middle School (MAGRES)

AID India was also running a residential school for the dropouts in Thoothukudi district. thirty-six children were given training and education and they were put in the regular schools after the completion of the ten-month basic residential course. Unfortunately this is not running any more.

AID India's general secretary, Mr. S. Peter Raj, also founded a school for low-caste children, namely Maria Grace Middle School. I went there in order to give English courses to the teachers who, although English is an official language in India, very often don't know how to write and speak properly (even if they have to teach it to the students). Consequently, I set up a program according to their needs and level of English[17]. It now became a high school.

e. She Home

AID India was taking care of sixteen girls in 2007, eighteen in 2019, who could not get education because of their family's poverty or because they were deserted by their parents. They are in the "She Home" and feel as if they are in their home. The home is functioning near the school as Ave Maria Home for children.

I had the opportunity to see them often since I was living very close. It is residential, and all facilities including food and accommodation are freely given. Previously there were twenty-eight girls, but unfortunately the NGO could not afford the money for all of them.

f. Match Industry run by MARIA

The match industry in Virudhunagar was successful and the members were very happy to run it. But unfortunately on July 12th 2007 there was a fire accident and the factory was totally destroyed, as I noted when I visited the site. AID India obtained from the Rabobank Foundation the cancellation of the debt for the loans. The NGO tried to find an alternative for the members affected by this accident. The problem is now solved.

g. Awareness on the Right to Information Act 2005

As an example of the collaboration with AVE MARIA once more, AID India conducted many camps and training sessions to give awareness on the Right to Information Act 2005. A number of teachers and students have been getting

---

[17] Cf. Teaching program and examples of the essay I made them write, in the annex A

benefits from this program. That is why AID India supported AVE MARIA in the publication of *Energy* magazine. I could see how the awareness program was important in the functioning of the different programs AID India was running.

h. Other Regular Programs

The other regular programs are Community-Based Rehabilitation for the people with disabilities, vocational training program in tailoring for the Dalit girls and also the promotion of humanist Self-Help Groups (SHG) in different places. A tailoring course has been conducted in three villages with thirty girls in each one. The Community-Based Rehabilitation program is closely related to the microcredit program, which is also addressed to the persons with disabilities and Dalit people.

i. Humanist Centers

The NGO also established twenty-one humanist centers. Each center is the place for the children to get a place for study in the evening. And it is a place for the women and other villagers for common discussion and meetings. One important project was the school's building, which would also serve as a Humanist center for the other people living in the village. This project was sent to the NGO's contacts in Berkeley University, USU, who were interested in helping and had asked for a project of that kind.

j. Tamilnadu Farm

In this farm, banana plants and coconut trees are cultivated. I didn't have the opportunity to see that project closely, but there was a direct link with the other projects, since the income the NGO gets from the farm is diverted to the homes for children and the programs for People with Disabilities (PWDs). This farm is still trying to find support to become a research center or a model farm for farmers. The NGO was also planning to establish a dairy farm. The NGO still needs funds, since the dairy farm is not yet established.

k. Penpal Program, Website

This penpal program, for the children adopted and for the children in the homes, had been designed by Emmi Beck, USA, who was organizing the letters. The US children and the Indian children were exchanging letters. This program was useful for cultural exchange and for twining the children in the right way. Also AID India's website was maintained by Emmi Beck by means of regular payment for the domain. This program is not handled by E. Beck any more.

l. Microcredit Program (Grama Vasantham)

The main program I could evaluate closely is the microcredit program. Its name, "Grama Vasantham", means "village prosperity". This program is conducted for the socio-economic development of the less-privileged communities. It gives sustainable development for independent living. Women and people with disabilities (PWDs) are organized in Self-Help Groups (SHG) for a better and efficient involvement in this program.

Indeed, giving credit is giving a wonderful opportunity to the poor, to explore fully their potential, and use their skills and talents for productive purposes, for themselves and at the same time for the welfare of their society and country. As I could see through my experience on the grassroots level, the only thing they lack is a small amount of capital to start their business. There are many ways they can do it: making clothes, baskets, repairing bikes, cultivating fruits or vegetables, herding goats, cows, chickens, or through various services such as rickshaw transportation, newspapers distribution, or any other businesses like selling food/drinks or clothes etc.If loans are first given to women[18], this is not at all a coincidence. As a matter of fact, women are the ones who suffer the most from poverty. If one of the family members has to starve, this is always women, who feed, as I could see by myself, men and children first. Women, who are proved to be the most concerned by the family's well-being, are much better fighters than men to move up, with an incredibly dignity, force and sense of sac-

---

[18] Cf. my report about the forum between the Tamil government, a bank and SHGs in the annex B

rifice, especially for their children's future. This is why most of the beneficiaries (more than eighty percent) are women - others being the people with disabilities, who are also disregarded and very hard-working and motivated to become independent. Therefore, credit constitutes a fundamental human right. It does not only create self- employment but also give women (and PWDs) self-confidence and in the meantime consideration and respect from their family and husband, while the situation in India always puts them into the background (with a major difference in the way they are raised - very often no education and a less qualitative food, with a very high rate of abortions and all kinds of crimes committed against women who are only socially and administratively recognized as "daughter" or "wife of" etc.). Thus, as Prof. Yunus insists, "by removing poverty, not only do we remove hunger, we also ensure other human rights - right for shelter, education, health and political freedom"[19].

---

[19] YUNUS Muhammad, *Acceptance speech at the award ceremony of the World Food Price*, December 1994

PART II: The microcredit program's effectiveness and Self-Help Groups

One of the main programs is Grama Vasantham, the microcredit program settled by AID India (Action In Disabilities India) in April 2000. In the regional language "grama" means "village" and "vasantham" means "prosperity" or "spring season". In the spring season, people are happy and joyful. Thus, the name "Grama Vasantham" denotes a desirable improvement or joyful state, because it allows the upliftment of people so that their life remains an eternal spring. To be more precise, this program aims at decrease of poverty for the poorest of the poor, in particular low-caste women and people with disabilities (PWDs). Thanks to income generating activities orientated to the local market, the excluded have the possibility to express their knowledge and create their own activity. Through this, they have more consideration and respect inside their family and community. Therefore, the economic and social consequences are extremely positive.

Grama Vasantham microcredit program is based on the Grameen Bank model.

I. Grama Vasantham microcredit program

In the Grama Vasantham program, to get a loan, groups of five (for disabled) or ten (for women) people at least have to be formed, and twenty at the most (which is quite different from Prof. M. Yunus' original model, because of the local constraints which force the NGO to pay for bigger groups). These five/ten members minimum should come from the same village and have similar living conditions. Groups work in a democratic way and responsibilities are collectively shared.

Indeed, each member participates actively to the program, which is essential since the purpose is also to give them strength and self-confidence. A meeting is fixed each month, during which all the Self-Help Group (SHG) members and a member of the NGO's staff meet in order to repay the loans, interests and the mandatory savings. This meeting is a special moment to create strong links between members, who will be able to be heard more effectively in public or private institutions.

In 2007, thirty-two people were working at AID India[20], among which fifteen in this program of microcredit. They were all coming from Satankulam or around, and knew precisely the specific problems in this area, and also all the population's traditions. Besides, the staff was much experienced as, before coming in this program, the field workers had at least a three years experience in a charitable organization. Moreover, all members attended trainings at least six times a year.

In 2007, the program counted 6,190 beneficiaries, coming from villages in four different districts (Thoothukudi, Tirunelveli, Kanyakumari, Virudhunagar), in a diameter of two hundred kilometres around the block of Satankulam where the headquarter of the organization is. I had the chance to visit many of them, in order to be able to understand the microcredit system better, and that

---

[20] Cf. AID India's website www.humanistaidindia.org

is what I am going to try to explain in this part. Now, most of them became independent, and the government undertook the same program.

A) The program's background

As I said previously the people's living conditions are extremely difficult, both on the economic and social aspects, and especially for women and people with disabilities. This is only after analyzing it that the NGO came up to the conclusion that something had to be done.

1. In general:

The area the NGOs work in is one of the poorest areas in India. Indeed it is very drought, and the rain is not sufficient to provide enough jobs in the agriculture. The failure of monsoon limits the agricultural development. An agricultural coolie is earning very few money. Since it is near the seashore, fishing becomes the livelihood of many people, even if it is a very dangerous and hazardous work. Moreover, the area was in 2007 still severely affected by the tsunami, which flushed everything away, including the fauna and flora necessary for good harvests. It is now all right in 2020. The other job opportunities are construction of buildings, brick making or bidis cigarettes' rolling. However, the local population suffers from the lack of job opportunities, which would provide them a regular income.

2. The social problems:

The targeting region is a remote area and consequently there is a lack of transport, health and educational facilities.

Especially the situation of the children is dramatic, since a lot of them have never entered a school. Actually, the educational costs are too high for the parents who are struggling to earn their living. Besides, due to a lack of awareness and education, they do not clearly see the usefulness of sending their children to school. Thus, child labor exists and is a concerning issue.

3. The economical problems:

In India, people are facing another problem when they want to borrow money. The only means for them is getting loans from private money lenders at a high interest rate. This interest rate ranges from sixty to 120 percent In some villages the interest rate can be higher than this. People get loans from them mortgaging their assets and at last they lose their assets too. The money lenders get their signature at the outset on a plain document paper. If the loans are not repaid properly in time as agreed, the assets are seized and will never be given back. Even if they are capable of repaying the loans to them, the interest to be paid until the final settlement is very high and it will totally exceed the capital amount in large.

B) The program's description:

The description made above clearly highlights that the living conditions of people were unacceptable and that measures had to be taken in order to improve their life and bring them to the main stream. This is why AID India decided seven years ago to implement the Grama Vasantham microcredit program.

1. How to contract a loan? Components:

This microcredit program was created as a replication of the program created by the Grameen bank in Bangladesh. AID India's general secretary, Mr. S. Peter Raj, attended a training in Bangladesh with Nobel Prize-winner Prof. Yunus, in order to replicate the Grameen bank program in the targeting area around Satankulam.

First, the staff members of Grama Vasantham, who are the field workers, identify women or PWDs in villages (who are the most disadvantaged people and therefore the ones the program is addressed to), and draw the list of the persons with all the details requested about their situation. Then the procedures of the program are explained to them. If they are prepared to join, the scheme training is arranged for them (usually during five days) to make sure they understand the program thoroughly. On the last day, they are asked to fill in the form for admission to the scheme and will open an account in the local bank. Thus the group is recognized by Grama Vasantham. Before getting a loan, the members will have to pay regularly the mandatory savings during twenty-five weeks (six months). After this period, which will serve as a test, they will be able to ask for a loan.

In a group, the number of members is fixed at five (for disabled) or ten (for women) persons minimum to twenty maximum, and it is strictly followed. The group is formed with people coming from the same village, who know and trust each other. But for the disabled, they may come from different villages (close to each other), it all depends on the number of disabled the village counts.

Groups work in a democratic way and responsibilities are collectively shared. Indeed, each member participates actively to the program, which is essential since the program intends to give them strength and self-confidence. If they meet some difficulties, they talk about it within the group and take their own decisions, which they write down in the appropriate notebook, different from the one where the account details are. In case of conflict, the group's leader decides.

Meetings between the group and one of AID India's field workers are conducted monthly, according to the convenience and decision of the group's members. This is the moment when people repay the principal of their loan and the compulsory savings, which is reported in their individual passbook[21]. Savings were usually around fifty rupees per month and person. But for persons in a critical situation, the amount of the savings can be more or less. As a result, the program is flexible and adapted to each situation in order to meet the specific needs of everyone. Besides, these meetings are special moments to share ideas and express the difficulties met in the income generating activities as well as in the family or community. This is essential that poor people gather and form a united block. In that way, they will be able to be heard more effectively in public or private institutions, and will not stay excluded from the society.

The staff comes for the repayment, but also to encourage and advise the members. They repeat the basic information about education, hygiene, health, nutrition, and human rights, in order that their socio-economic conditions are improved efficiently and durably. The staff members also meet once a month in order to take stock of the situation[22] in the different villages the NGO works in.

1. The current situation

In 2007, AID India had 6,190 members. According to the report realized on March 31st, 2007, the total amount of loan given reaches Rs 5,850,000 and the total of outstanding loan Rs 6,658,208. The total savings mobilized is Rs 6,501,910.

The amount of the loan depends on the need and the business. The average of loan was six thousand rupees, as the minimum loan size is four thousand rupees and the maximum is ten thousand rupees. The loan size has to be decided by the group members only. Clients may obtain a second loan with the group's agreement and Grama Vasantham's staff. Indeed, if one repays his/her first loan every month seriously and his/her activity is successful, the group often agrees to help the member in the development of his/her activity.

---

[21] Cf. individual passbook, one of the eight notebooks for the SHGs, and translation of the rules and oath in the annex C

[22] Cf. report of the staff meeting in the annex D

Besides, AID India is on a good way to become independent. Indeed, the strategy is to let the program grow, so that it can reach a sufficient size. Therefore, all costs related to the functioning of the organization, as administrative fees and salaries are not deducted from the profit generated by the program but are met by AID India organization. The loan rate is fifteen percent approximately (according to the group leader's decision), as the NGO borrows to the local bank at a rate which varies between ten percent and 13.5 percent.

The mandatory savings' system, of which the amount is fixed unanimously by the group (which was around fifty rupees permonth and person), is essential for the clients. As a matter of fact, they can use it for the internal loans (the first loans serving as a test). They are also able to forecast their future expenses for marriages, festivals, dowry, etc., which are very high in India. They can also protect themselves against risks, accidents, climate hazards. They have the possibility to have liquidities during the slack periods. Finally, there is a tied link between savings and education, since thanks to savings, children will be able to go to school for a longer period. Education and fighting against child labor is one of AID India's priorities, and Grama Vasantham can contribute in an efficient way to that goal.

For Grama Vasantham, savings are essential to become independent. Indeed, thanks to savings, the organization will be able to reduce the risks of illiquidity, and beneficiate from regular income without needing to call for silent partners.

At last, we can say that repayment rate is almost perfect with ninety-nine percent (in 2007, the main cause of failure was due to the tsunami in 2004 which flushed everything away and left clients without jobs and in the incapacity to repay loans and interests. It is now OK.). If someone is not able to pay back on time, the rest of the group pays for that member temporarily, because there is a strong solidarity. Moreover, people are very motivated to get to the main stream. Therefore, non-repayment is extremely rare.

2. The different activities

Women and people with disabilities (PWDs) get micro-loans in order to establish a small activity, which will enable them to generate regular income. They choose their activity by their own, according to their capacities and skills. If there is a specific need in the area (as clothes, baskets or local products making), AID India takes charge of their training. Thus, they can realize this specific activity and sell the products needed by the local population. Different activities are possible:

- Clothes, baskets etc. making...
- Bikes repair...
- Agriculture (vegetables, fruits...)
- Goats, cows, chickens herding...
- Various services as rickshaw transportation, newspaper distribution...
- Businesses selling food/drinks (tea, coffee, fruit juice), clothes...

3. The main goals

Since its inception, AID India was working to erase poverty among the most needy. Indeed, the main goals were:

- To broaden the program in a durable way in all Tamilnadu state
- To send all members' children to school (at least until thirteen years-old) and no longer in factories or fields, and develop the school created by AID India's general secretary, Mr. Peter Raj, to enable all children to have access to higher secondary schools.
- To deliver two thousand loans per year, which will prevent families to ask private money lenders
- To improve social status of women and PWDs within their home, but also village and community

• To create strong links between members so that they can defend their interests in both private and governmental institutions

Now it has been taken over by the government.

4. The outcomes and case stories

a. The visible results:

This program has a lot of positive outcomes in the economical, social and psychological development of the area. Here are some of these outcomes:

• Loans provide families with regular and sustainable incomes
• People can afford three meals per day
• Child labor is decreasing
• Literacy rate is increasing
• People do not have to go to private lenders who levy high interest rates (from sixty to 120 percent)
• The social status of women is improving, they are better regarded by their husband
• In the case of disabled people, they can gain self-esteem and forget their disability in mingling with others
• There is a better integration in families, communities and villages
• There is also a growing awareness on several subjects like rights, education, health, nutrition
• Future hope is strongly established.

b. Three case stories:

We can give three examples of activities, set up by the beneficiaries:

1. LOURDU MARY, Dalit woman: snacks selling

Lourdu Mary was aged thirty-five years and lived in Fatimanagar, India. Her family consisted of her husband and four children. She had no regular income and she had no capital for investment in a business. She could not send her children to school due to poverty prevailing in the family.

Before starting her business she had to live on the meager wages that was brought by her husband. It was not enough for pulling on the family. She joined a Grama Vasantham SHG and made regular savings along with the other members. The center decided to give her a loan of five thousand rupees for her snacks business (as she had interest in preparation of various snacks including sweets and cookies). She got it and purchased the materials required to start her business. She now gets bulk order from groups and marriage parties. Further, her husband cooperates in the business and he sells the sweets and other items in the streets every day. Thus, she gets a regular and average net profit of one hundred rupees a day.

2. PETER, disabled: book binding

Peter, who was forty years, was disabled because of a polio attack. He was moving thanks to a tricycle. He was not yet married, and living alone in Udangudi, India. But he was also very strong-minded.

Before starting this work, he had no business and no income for living. Though he had his own house, he struggled hard for food. He got loans from private groups for his expenses. But the people who gave him money scolded him for not paying it back. At that juncture, the staff members of Grama Vasantham (MCP) met him and explained him the program. Consequently he joined a Grama Vasantham group and made regular savings along with the other members. The group decided to give him a loan of ten thousand rupees for his book binding business. He bought all the tools like the cutting machine with the money and he took bulk order from a printing press and separate orders from students. He is now binding books for printing presses and for the student community, and gets a regular income of one hundred rupees a day.

3. ARUMUGAM, widow and disabled: mat weaving

Arumugam, who was forty-two years old, was both widow and disabled, due to rheumatic fever in her childhood. She was living in Pettaikulam, India. She was alone, since she only had a sister, who was living in another village.

Before starting her business she had difficulties in making her living happy. She had no job opportunity. Occasionally, she got a job and with the meager wages she got from the job, she pulled on her life. She joined a SHG for disabled and started to make regular savings at the same time as the other members. On her request and as per the resolutions passed in the group, she got a loan of five thousand rupees for her mat weaving business. After attending a training on mat weaving, and with this money, she purchased raw materials for mat weaving. She now gets bulk order from businessmen. This product is for making parcels of jaggery, tamarind etc. Marketing is easy for her. The business people come to her house directly every week and purchase the finished products. Thus, she gets regular income through this business. In the meantime she is making savings too. And she is able to honour her debts perfectly.

Thus, the results of the program are very positive, even if changes occur slowly. Indeed, evaluating the modifications in mentalities and traditions is a work difficult to realize. However, the staff is very close to the clients and meets them regularly. They talk a lot with the members and therefore, are able to assess the evolutions in habits. Besides, they control very frequently whether members are respecting the rules of the program: for example, if they don't borrow money from private money lenders, and if they send their children to school regularly. If the field workers find out that the rules are infringed, they ask for explanations from the members and demand that they rectify their mistakes, explaining them that it is in their own interest.

There are many problems which can emerge. But with the staff's experience and the strong links they weaved with the members, they adapt the program and solve the problems. To give an example, if a member wants to obtain a loan for fruit trees' plantation, he/she has to have established another income generating activity. Indeed, the climate conditions in the region are very uncertain, and depending on the years, the harvest will be more or less good. In order to secure the repayment of the loan, another activity is therefore mandatory.

II. Women, second class citizens, but pillars of the family

If microcredit was first addressed to women, this is not a coincidence. According to the National Family Health Survey-4 (NFHS-4) in India, the proportion of women with no education is thirty-one percent (fifteen percent for males), twenty-nine percent of married women suffer spousal abuse and many of them feel it is justifiable. The women's status is still suffering. For Elizabeth Bumiller, Washington bureau chief for the *New York Times* who came and travelled all over India, having a girl is considered as a shame and besides getting married, the only thing a girl can hope for, is carrying a boy, otherwise in many cases, and especially if she and her husband had one or two girls before, they will just decide to kill her (if they didn't use the prenatal medical techniques as a sex test to practice abortion in case it is a girl)[23]. Sex-selective abortion is still a reality. Women's very hard situation is something we can notice, with many cases of destitute women, girls left to child labor (because they don't deserve school since they will be married as soon as possible), women burnt alive (in many cases because their husband or his family don't want her any more, or sometimes even because she delivered a girl - regardless of the female sexual gene's paternal transmission, because of their ignorance). For many of the people, "the worse of the two evils (between dying or living as a girl) is the state that a woman is

---

[23] BUMILLER Elizabeth, *May you be the mother of a hundred sons*, N.Y: Random House, 1990, 220p

going to face until the day she dies"[24]. I had the opportunity to visit many villages and talk to many people, especially women, and I saw the despair of their situation, even if they do accept it, but I also saw how strong and determined the women were. They were waiting for, somehow, to get to the mainstream. Giving them this chance is the best way to achieve it, because while too many men still consume their despair (and money) in alcohol, women are proved to be the best persons to trust in improving the family's living conditions, at the same time they are improving their own social status…

A) The situation of women:

Although women are discredited in a society that only values men, with a crime rate dramatically high, women are capital assets for a country, as they usually possess the qualities (maybe precisely because of their status) to improve the socio- economic conditions of their families.

1. In general:

The situation of women in India, and especially low-caste women like the dahlits, is alarming. The social cause for their low status starts at birth or even before birth. They are treated as inferior, their self-esteem is very low, and they become like slaves in society. All components of their health (physical, psychological, social, economical and spiritual) are neglected. Society exploits them at every turn and often they are denied good nutrition, education and the right to a well remunerated employment.

2. Some key figures:

According to the National Crime Records Bureau, violence on women has increased in the last few years. The rate of crime against women – crimes per

---

[24] Idem.

hundred thousand female population – was 55.2 in 2016 (up from 41.7 in 2012). As many as 2.5 million crimes against women have been reported in India over the last decade. Reported cases of crime against women increased eighty-three percent from 185,312 in 2007 to 338,954 in 2016. "Cruelty by husband or his relatives" was the most reported crime against women, accounting for thirty-three percent of all crimes in 2016 – 110,378 cases or thirteen crimes every hour. The number of rapes and murders against women are very important too.

3. Women, persons of merit:

Nevertheless, women can be considered as the greatest asset of society. They spend their life working for the welfare and prosperity of their families. There is an Indian folk proverb that illustrates the important role of women in society "The father of a daughter will never go hungry" and also "Behind every successful man, there is a woman". Indeed, women cook, have knowledge in indigenous plants and medicines, and are repository of religious life. They are very creative and express their talents in art and craft. Moreover, they contribute to the durability of society in giving birth. It is important to highlight that their health affects the health of future citizens of India. Therefore it is crucial to take care of them and show that they are an essential link in a thriving society.

B) The projects for women and their children

Although microcredit is addressed to women, there is no microcredit project without projects for their children, who are usually the main concern for them. Indeed, giving them self-employment gives them regular income which makes it easier to stop sending their children to work. Thus, microcredit is also a solution to eliminate child labor. However, this is not sufficient enough, since proper measure has to be taken (especially infrastructure) for the children's education and their well-being.

1. A typical project for women

In Tamilnadu state, and in particular in the districts taken care of by AID India, fishing is the main business for the people. Their fishing vehicle is called kattamara. They sail to distant place in the sea, to have good harvest. But that kind of fishing is not so lucrative. Some people use engines for the kattamara. But only forty percent machineries are available. Fishing is also depending on the season, wind and other climatic aspects. If the climate is good, they get plenty of shrimps. Otherwise, they get different varieties of fish. Shrimp can be exported to other countries too. In 2007 they did not get good harvest because of the tsunami, which flashed everything away, but is now over. They do not have training in other businesses.

The fishes they can get give them small profit. Sometimes they embrace heavy loss in fishing, their business is volatile. Now they are poorer than other communities who are living far from sea. Thus, the people living in this area were needing an urgent support.

As the results of the Grama Vasantham (GV) program was extremely positive, it was meaningful to help them through the formation of SHGs, providing them with loans and trainings to start income generating activities. It is also important to underline that with the constitution of women and PWD groups, all the community could benefit from this help. But, if some people were already beneficiaries, others needed the help of the program.

Although there were many projects for women, I evaluated a few of them for children, because in those programs everything has to be considered altogether, especially issues concerning children, given that they will be the future citizens of the country who will make changes possible.

2. And some projects for their children

Besides the microcredit projects, AID India is running many other projects. As a matter of fact, all of them are indivisible because, concerning development issues, all aspects should be considered at the same time. That is why AID India also founded an orphanage, namely Island of Hope, and a Home for girls called "She Home". The organization also decided to run a distance adoption program (also called sponsorship program) with its partners in other countries, and distribute clothes to the less-privileged children (that is to say the children of the women, who are taking part in the Grama Vasantham program).

a. Project for the orphans

General information about Island of Hope orphanage

One of the projects undertaken by AID India is Island of Hope orphanage, in Virudhunagar. Initiated by Narovinu, Czech Republic, this orphanage was being run by AID India with 102 children in 2007, only fifty by the end of 2019. In 2007 the third floor construction was finished and it is now used as a study hall and library for the children. As I said previously, the aim of this orphanage is to bring up the children in a humanist way.

The geographical area of the project

Island of Hope orphanage was built in 2005, with the Czech government humanitarian support, through Narovinu humanistic center in Czech Republic.

It is located in Virudhunagar district, which is in Tamilnadu state, India. In 2007, a large part of the children were directly or indirectly touched by the tsunami, which is not the case anymore. But the profile is the same: they are either full orphans, semi orphans or deserted by their parents. All are from very low caste families, and thus not able to supply food and education.

Without this orphanage, those children would have stayed in the rural and remote areas and become child laborers, or street children. As an example, one of the children was found in a dustbin in the area of Paramakudi. Thus, Virudhunagar was chosen for the location of the orphanage as it can provide facilities such as a school and colleges with technical institutions, and as it is also a city of job opportunities.

The present needs in Island of Hope orphanage

I noticed there were three needs in Island of Hope orphanage:

• *Kitchen Garden and Poultry:* The total area available for the kitchen garden is 13579.025 ft^2 (1261.532 m^2). AID India had finished building the bath facility in the land, to make it a kitchen garden for the orphanage. AID India is still looking for financial support for this project.

There are possibilities of growing greens/cabbages in the small garden. The water coming from the bath tub can go to the plants in the garden.

A small poultry with one hundred chickens is possible. In this way, the orphanage can get eggs regularly. After getting sufficient eggs from the chicken, it can become meat for the children. The dung of the poultry unit can also be utilized as natural manure for the plants in the garden.

The kitchen garden and poultry can give greens and eggs permanently. The children can also be involved in the unit. It is interesting for them and can become like a hobby to the children. In the day time, the staff can take care of the unit.

• *Sponsorship:* In 2007, as per the agreement, eighty children in the orphanage have been sponsored by Narovinu. Of the remaining, fifteen children have been adopted by SOS Diritti Umani and the other seven children are waiting for sponsors. Well-wishers have now started sponsoring the children one by one. The orphanage can accommodate totally 120 children. If more children are adopted, they will stay in this home. Adoptions are still going on.

•

• *Bathrooms:* This was one the most critical problem the orphanage was facing and trying to deal with. As a matter of fact, the children in the orphanage could not take their bath properly. The first problem was there were only six toilets and six showers for 102 children, which was a very difficult situation to handle. The second major and very critical problem was the evacuation of the worn waters. As they (the orphanage run by AID India) could not be connected with the main canal of drainage, they made a big pit underground and, as usually, started using the drainage facility. But the tank was full with drainage. So, as the orphanage didn't have enough money for a canal, they fixed a motor to eliminate the wastages and let the drainage go into the vacant adjacent land. But this was only a temporary solution and the owner of that land started of course to make complaints. AID India managed to find funds to build bathroom facilities at a distant place, but the problem for toilets was still there, and the waste waters were still going to that land. Besides, because of the nature of the soil, water was not absorbed after it was raining, and there was then another major problem with stagnant waters, which could cause as one knows many diseases (carried by mosquitoes), and provoke many accidents with the proximity of electric poles etc. Hence, the hygiene of the place and security of our children was not sure anymore.

The urgency of the problem and the project proposal

Therefore, there was a major and urgent problem concerning the bathrooms in the orphanage:

1) The problem of the soil and the temporary solution

At the time of the construction, AID India did not know about the nature of the soil. Also the people there did not know about the drainage problem. Since the orphanage was a little bit away from the main streets of the city and since they were under the control of the village administration (though it was near the new main bus station of Virudhunagar), they could not be connected with the main canal of drainage. They made a big pit underground and as usually started using the drainage facility, which was perfect for six months. But unfortunately it created problems after six months. The tank was full with drainage, so they fixed a motor to eliminate the wastages. Since the adjacent land was vacant they let the drainage go into the land. The problem was a little bit solved by this, but just temporarily.

2) The land spoilt belonging to another owner

The owner of the land, where the drainage was going to, happened to be a doctor. He became furious and scolded them. He went to the extent of making a complaint against the orphanage in the police station. Then the orphanage approached the government to solve the problem. And they were then still trying to deal with the problem.

3) The problem of bath facilities

In the meantime the problem became acute. Hence, AID India decided to make arrangements for bathing in the nearby land, which was owned by the organization. On this land, it erected a small room for getting a door number for domicile so that it could apply for power connection. The organization again applied for it. It needed to have two electric posts for connection. AID India managed to get them, and finally the orphanage had connection. Earlier AID India had made a bore-well to have more water. This water was softer compared to the water available in the present home. The organization bought a submersible motor and was relieved because the water was good for taking bath and for washing clothes.

Children were happy to come to this place to take bath. But they found no closed place for taking bath. The NGO planned to establish a big tub and a closed place for taking bath. As per the plan, the children could take bath together around the big tub. Now the construction is done. But the NGO could not wait for assistance from other agencies, since it was a serious problem connected to the day-to-day life of the children staying there. The organization provided buckets for taking bath and then the boys and girls were taking bath separately every day in the morning and on holidays they made use of the place for washing. But this was also a temporary solution, as it was not easy for them to reach that place every morning. So the main idea was to enable them to come back to the orphanage to take their bath, and build another floor for the bathrooms since there were only six toilets and six showers for the 102 children.

4) The hygiene and danger of the situation

But though the NGO found a momentary solution for the children to take their bath in a distant place, and though it is not an easy situation for them, there was still the problem for the toilets.

The waste waters were still going to the neighbor's land, which was a double problem:

• first because the owner was of course very unhappy with it and was wishing to give some judicial problems (even if AID India was not itself satisfied of this situation and didn't know how to deal with it, since it didn't have the money).

• second because this caused a major problem of insalubrity and hygiene for the children and the staff living along with them.

Besides this, the nature of the soil didn't absorb the water each time it was raining, even if rain is rare. Consequently, there were always stagnant waters around the orphanage. This constituted a major issue, since stagnant waters attract mosquitoes, carrying many diseases, which could become very dangerous for the 102 children living there in 2007 (fifty by the end of 2019). And mosquito diseases are not uncommon in the region, as there are many cases of chikungunya and malaria, among others. This was even more dangerous, as there were some electric poles going along the road in front of the orphanage. In case of a storm, which also happened sometimes (although it was also rare), this situation could also be extremely dangerous, as water was just under the electric poles.

As a temporary solution, the organization managed to raise the level of the ground on the left of the orphanage, where the toilets and the prior bathrooms were, which also enabled the orphanage to dry the clothes in that area and became a small playground for the children. But this was only temporary and the problem of evacuating the waters, first the waste ones, and the others, was still there, for the hygiene and also security and safety of the children, to ensure they live in a neat place.

Strategy and budget to achieve the project purpose
Consequently, there were two parts in that project.

First, it would urgently need to get the facilities in the orphanage by making a canal from the toilets to the main canal of the city. It assumed a participation of the NGO at least to the extent of fifty percent of the total cost. The total cost was 180,000 rupees. So the NGO needed to meet half of the amount – ninety thousand rupees.

Second, once the canal problem was solved, another floor for the bathrooms could be built (as there were only six toilets and six showers), and be connected to this canal. This would be of a total cost of 199,980 rupees.

These were the actual expenses for the project which was sent to many organizations and groups, in particular three Medical groups from Creighton University (USA) who came over summers. As it was related to health and directly affecting the living conditions of the children who should live at least in a hygienic and secure place, people related to the medical field could indeed be the best partners to talk to. Unfortunately nothing happened.

b. Project for the orphans and the beneficiaries' children

Other projects undertaken by AID India and beneficiaries of the project proposal
All the projects, including the ones for childhood development, are located in Tamilnadu state, India. A large part of the children were in 2007 directly or indirectly touched by the tsunami (it is not the case anymore), all from very low caste families, and thus not able to supply food, education and proper clothes.

Therefore, providing them with all kinds of facilities was a priority: food and education through sponsorship programs and proper clothes every year at Christmas through grants.

1. Children in the poor villages of the area

In 2007 AID India adopted through the sponsorship program *192 children* in the four districts thanks to SOS Diritti Umani organization. Previously they were 210, but some people withdrew their support. The children are supported in their educational needs. Also the community the children live in are benefitting from this program by means of independent living through sustainable businesses. Child development centers and special tuition for the children are some of the programs to lift the children. The sponsorship program is still going on.

2. Children in Island of Hope

Another project undertaken by AID India, of which I talked about, is Island of Hope Orphanage, in Virudhunagar. Initiated by Narovinu, Czech Republic, this orphanage were counting 102 children in 2007, fifty by the end of 2019.

Ninety-six children of them were adopted through sponsorships in 2007 and is still counting on sponsorship. The orphanage can accommodate totally 120 children. So if more children are adopted, they will stay in this home.

3. Children in She Home

In 2007 sixteen girls (eighteen in 2019), who could not get education because of poverty in the family and because of being deserted by their parents are in the 'She Home'. Just like in Island of Hope, they also feel they are in their home. Previously there were twenty-eight girls, but unfortunately it was not possible for the NGO to afford the money for all of them.

The families of these children could not afford new clothes for them, which is a very difficult problem as they need to have proper clothes since they are still growing. Therefore, each year, the NGO were organizing a program and asking for grants in order to supply them with clothes for Christmas.

As a matter of fact, this project has to be sent early enough in order to find grants.

c. Project for the beneficiaries' children

Need of the project and beneficiaries

Valan Nagar village comes under Kanyakumari district, in the very south of Tamilnadu. There again, a large part of the children were in 2007 affected by the tsunami, since parents were almost all involved in fishing. Again, all are from very low-caste families, and thus not able to supply them with proper education.

Moreover, while the parents go to work, the children are often left by themselves. The other problem is that if the school is far from the village, parents will not let the children to go to school as they don't have the money to pay for busses.

So AID India was organizing classes in a rented building, but the cost was so high that it was extremely difficult to continue that way. This is why, since the NGO owned some land, the organization was willing to build a school on that site.

The building would not only serve for the *school classes*, but also for all kind of important *meetings* in the villages, such as the ones which attend the village's Self-Help Groups each month for the microcredit program.

At that time, since they didn't have proper place to do so, the members along with the staff had to meet in the middle of the street which was very uncomfortable for them, as this street is the main one in the village and people were coming from one side or another.

Moreover, this building would be a perfect place for them to get trainings in other trades than fishing, since after the tsunami it was very difficult for them to handle the situation as they were running out of fishes.

Through this, the husbands would be able to continue fishing while the women would start running new businesses and make sure they diversify their activities. Also, the building could serve for men as a place for discussions.

In the end, something was built. This building was conceived as a community hall/humanist center since, besides the classes in the day, it would also serve for many different activities.

III. The particular case of people with disabilities

As most of the families are poor, the family members think that the people with disabilities are burdens to the families. They discard them in the day-to-day life. More preference is given to the so-called "normal people". If the disabled is a girl, the situation becomes deplorable. She has two disabilities – by being a girl she is already disabled! No one will come forward to marry them. She will be more or less abandoned. People think that education is not needed for the ones who are seen as a "useless community". And since most of the disabled do not have income, they do not get care and attention from the family.

A) The situation of people with disabilities:

People with disabilities always suffer from discrimination. In a country where poverty affects half a billion people, they are considered, just like women, as another burden to the family. This is regardless of their capacities and talents which, if they have the chance to use them in particular through income generating activities, can also benefit to their own family.

1. In general:

In India, people with disabilities are regarded as useless, they are rejected by the society and consequently do not have access to basic facilities. Poverty does not allow them to plan for their future, and their parents usually give preference for education to the "normal" children, especially boys (who are the ones suposed to take care of them when they are old). In the 2011 Census[25], the proportion of people living with disabilities was put at 2.21% of the population (but data can be questioned, when compared to the global average of fifteen percent). Most of the disabled (sixty-nine percent) reside in rural areas (just like the total population of India). But public identifies very few of them as disabled and has difficulties sorting out the disabled. And at the all-India level, only thirty-six percent of all disabled persons have a job.

Nevertheless, their situation must be improved; they do not have access to proper medical services, education, training or information. As per AID India's survey, only two or three percent of them have access to these services and ninety-five percent of the disabled live under the poverty line.

Without accurate data, the Indian government cannot effectively allocate resources for them. It does provide them with some support that is to say aids and appliances, scholarship, educational support. But practically these facilities cannot easily be obtained and people become weary of applying for. Indeed they have to submit a lot of certificates in order to be helped, and procedures take long time and are restricted.

---

[25] Census of India 2011 Data on Disability. Website: https://unstats.un.org/unsd/demographic-social/meetings/2016/bangkok--disability-measurement-and-statistics/Session-6/India.pdf

2. Results of a survey:

In order to have a clear vision of the situation of people with disabilities in the targeting area in Tamilnadu, AID India decided to carry out a survey. The results of this survey enable the NGO to know all details like age, sex, caste, religion, education qualification, kind of disability, reason for disability, family situation, economic background of the family, address, parents'/guardian's status etc[26].

AID India conducted this survey itself, using the resources of the staff members, local panchayat president, and the balwady (preschool) teacher. The helpers were equipped with proper training on the different kinds of disabilities to make this list meaningful and real.

3. The value of disabled people

Common misconceptions about the laziness of people with disabilities are utterly false. A lot of them want to mingle with other people forgetting their disabilities. They are motivated to have their own activity, which can help them meet their own needs and be a full part of the society.

To achieve this goal, that is to say to build a self-reliant and sustainable society, it seems very important to acknowledge that the work and the contribution of each person are essential. Everyone has its own role to play to improve society. Moreover, if some of them are neglected they will become a burden for the society and hinder its future development.

B) The projects for PWD

The microcredit program, aimed to the less privileged people, was a perfect way for PWDs to overcome their difficulties, both social and financial. In some villages, the program was urgent as there were a high number of PWDs who

---

[26] Cf. AID India's disabled group details in the annex E

needed help. However, the projects had to be adapted in such a way that it will also include the medical aspects to make their life better. That is why one of the projects was considering not only the credit aspect, but also their needs, and that is also why this kind of project requires more grants than loans (because it is more difficult for them than for people with a "normal" mobility to repay it).

1. The choice of the village to be taken care of

a. Geographical, socio-economic and religious background of the area

Geographical background

Periathalai is a village located in the seashore of the Bay of Bengal in South India. It comes under Thoothukudi district, Tamilnadu. The village is only seventy kilometres from Kanyakumari, where three seas (the Bay of Bengal, the Indian Ocean and the Arabian Sea) meet together. There is no river nearby. There are ups and downs on the surface, due to the wind. Sand is heaped then and there. Muthammalpuram and Michaelnagar are two smaller villages, which are included in this village.

Periathalai is eighteen kilometres from Satankulam where the headquarters of the office functions are, and which is also in Thoothukudi district.

Population and the Community

The population of this village is more than ten thousand inhabitants. As per the recent data collected by AID India, the village consists of many people with disabilities. The number the organization arrived at is around 435 (still around the same today). This attracted the NGO's attention. The majority of the disabled are girls, and most of them are orthopedically handicapped.

Religion and caste

Seventy-five percent of the population are fishermen. The name of their caste is *parava*. They belong to the Roman Catholic Church. They have been listed as *Most Backward Caste (MBC)* by the government.

The remaining population is belonging to the castes namely *parayan, pallan* and *saamban*. They belong to Hindu religion. They have been listed as *Scheduled Caste (SC)*. This particular community is also described as *Dalits*.

All castes in India are listed by the government. Indeed, the most disadvantaged castes are: *Forward Caste, Backward Caste, Most Backward Caste, Scheduled Caste (Dalits), and Scheduled Tribes*. The two last ones are called "untouchable". Therefore, the village is extremely poor.

Economic background of the village

Fishing is the main business for them, with their fishing vehicle: the "kattamara". Fishing is depending on climatic aspects. If the climate is good, they get eral fish (shrimp) in plenty. But it became less frequent and other kinds of fish give them a small profit. Even if they went to distant places in the sea by machine boats, they could get good harvests in 2007, especially because of the tsunami, which flushed everything away. And they do not have training in other businesses. They are usually poor communities, much more than other communities who are living far from sea.

Educational facilities

A Primary School and a High School are functioning in the village. Primary School is meant for the pupils between the age of five to ten, and the High School is for the pupils between the age of eleven and fifteen.

After completing the education in the school, the students have to aspire for higher studies in the Higher Secondary Schools, which are available in the towns. There is a Higher Secondary School in the nearby village namely Padukkapattu. But parents do not want to admit the students in the school, because it is a government school. Usually, the government schools do not give qualitative education. Hence the students have to go to distant places. Usually girls are dropouts in this stage. Very few boys, who can buy bicycles, can go to other towns for higher studies. And very few students go to cities and stay in the hostels for the higher studies.

b. AID India's intervention in the village and inclusion of the PWD in the microcredit program

AID India's intervention

AID India was forming Self-Help Groups (SHG) for the women members in the village. While the men are going to the sea for fishing, women members get loans for the fishing net, and thus the family could purchase new nets for their business. All family members involve in fishing in one way or another. Pre and post fishing jobs are assisted by the women in the families.

But the NGO also started forming SHGs for the people with disabilities. The Grama Vasantham microcredit program follows the same principles with some flexibility in number, age, sex etc., in the matter of people with disabilities. Since the families with disabled members have been severely affected, the NGO's attention has been diverted towards the development of the disabled. Through Grama Vasantham, AID India envisages possible training and income generating strategies for the disabled community.

Inclusion of the disabled in the microcredit program

Common aspects

This program admits all kinds of disabled irrespective of caste, creed, sex and religion, as a replication of Grameen Bank in Bangladesh founded by Prof. M. Yunus, from whom AID India's General Secretary had personal training.

Even the Minor disabled and Mentally Retarded (MR) are admitted in the program. In the case of Minors and MR, the responsibility should be taken by the parents or guardians. The parents/guardians should attend the meetings regularly. The entire responsibility is laid on them. They are fully eligible to take loans and remit the amounts on behalf of the disabled. When the children become grown-up, the saved amount may be spent for his/her welfare. When he/she becomes major, he/she (in the case of people with disabilities other than MR) becomes active in the Grama Vasantham program. In the case of MR, most of the parents' worries go around the thinking about the future position of the MR, after the death of the parents/guardians. Grama Vasantham is a solution for that, as it takes care of them, finding a suitable place for taking care of them until their end.

Number of members and particularities in forming a group

In the group, the number of members is fixed at a minimum of ten for women and five for the disabled, and a maximum of twenty for both. The group is formed with people coming from the same village, who know and trust each other.

But for the disabled, they may come from different villages (close to each other), depending on the number of disabled the village counts. Thus, in the case of People With Disabilities (PWDs), Grama Vasantham is not rigid in its rules and regulations with regard to the number and gender of the members, as per AID India's survey nearly ninety-five percent of the disabled live below poverty line. As a matter of fact, poverty is a source of amplification, if not the root, of their disability. However, some "economically sound" people are also disabled. So they are also admitted in this scheme, if they are willing to join it. Grama Vasantham aims at organizing all PWDs under one roof, so that it can find ways and means for the welfare of them altogether. As women groups, they can meet every month (according to their convenience and decision), and share their feelings during the meeting. A permanent relationship will be maintained among them through this scheme.

Amount of savings

As for women, the monthly compulsory savings (both individual and group savings) are not fixed. It may be variable according to the decision of the members, and vary from group to group. But once the amount is fixed for a particular group, that amount of savings fixed by the members should be followed by all the members uniformly. There should be no variation with regard to these savings in a particular group.

Loans for income generation

Grama Vasantham is giving proper training to PWDs, according to their physical fitness. After the completion of training, the disabled are allowed to take loans as they like, as per the decision of the concerned groups. The loans are utilized for the selected trade. When they begin to get regular income from the business, the loans are repaid in small installments spread in more months than for women, and which are fixed by the group only. As a matter of fact, there is no limit for them for repayments (as it is for women, fixed at thirty-six months).

Other programs given to the disabled

There are some other development programs in Grama Vasantham for the disabled, among which: referral services, guidance and counseling, skill training, treatment, health care, educational assistance, rehabilitation, preventive measures and awareness of disability. It is the entry point for the integration of the development programs for PWDs in the mainstream.

Disabled people in the administration

Each of Grama Vasantham groups has one animator. All the animators meet every six months, and they take decisions for the smooth and successful running of the program. These animators elect eight leaders unanimously among them. From these leaders, three are sent to the High level committee, which changes every year. In the High level committee, representation is given to the disabled leaders (as two leaders come from the women's groups and one

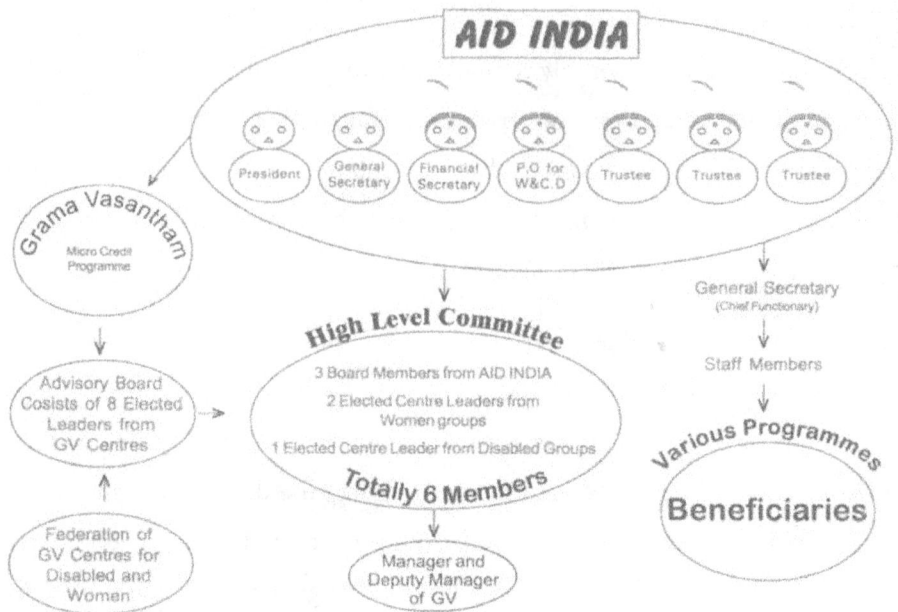

AID INDIA

President | General Secretary | Financial Secretary | P.O for W&C.D | Trustee | Trustee | Trustee

Grama Vasantham
Micro Credit Programme

General Secretary
(Chief Functionary)

High Level Committee

3 Board Members from AID INDIA
2 Elected Centre Leaders from Women groups
1 Elected Centre Leader from Disabled Groups

Staff Members

Advisory Board
Cosists of 8 Elected Leaders from GV Centres

Totally 6 Members

Various Programmes

Federation of GV Centres for Disabled and Women

Beneficiaries

Manager and Deputy Manager of GV

from the PWD's groups). Besides these three leaders, three board members are sent from AID India.

Therefore, there are six members in the Committee, among which two are chosen to be the manager and deputy manager (cf. the NGO's organigram above).

2. A typical project of microcredit for PWDs

One of the projects I assessed was concerning the PWDs. The budget was quite expensive but it was also very complete since it was trying to answer to all their needs. The specificities of this project, among which some aspects were essential to projects addressed to the PWDs, were the ones below.

a. The frequent meetings

Frequent contacts with the field officers

It is a strategy to get in touch with the PWDs and their parents/guardians. The background of the family is collected. Through these contacts, they become self-confident and feel more important. They are recognized through this.

Awareness meetings

Meetings are held for the PWDs and their parents/guardians in every street, so that the clients have access to attend the meetings without difficulties. In the meetings, awareness is given on education, health, treatment, preventive measures and government facilities due to them. Their rights are brought to light. They also have to be trained in getting the facilities (such as education, scholarships, obtaining identity cards, travel concessions, etc.) from the government.

Guidance and counseling

There should be a new office with a section for them for guidance and counseling, available both to the PWDs and their parents/guardians. One person with a master degree in education and teaching experience (who must have studied psychology or sociology as one of the subjects in his/her degree) should guide them in their needs.

b. Inclusive education, formation of SHGs for the disabled, and trainings

Inclusive education

The disabled children have to be put into the right schools, so that they can get education in the right age along with the "normal" children. Through this strategy, they will get education in the common platform. They will forget their disability and learn how to live in society.

Formation of SHGs

As mentioned above, AID India continuously form Self-Help Groups for the disabled community with flexible rules. In the group meetings, they start making savings for them. They are then able to get loans out of it. In the meantime they can share their ideas. They can fight, when they are deprived of their rights. They can also plan for the group ventures. They can discuss various issues affecting them and find possible solutions.

Awareness training to the school teachers in the area, and nutritious meals

If the school teachers are trained to identify the disabled and kinds of disability, they can cooperate with children and parents. Teachers and nutritious meal teachers should also be available in this area. They can be given training on this disability issue. This training can be given to the teachers working in the entire block of Satankulam, so they can learn how to cope with disabled children and how to support them in schools.

Leadership Training

Everyone have opportunities to become a leader in his/her group. But leaders should have some qualities, as they have more responsibilities in the group. They are models to the other members. Hence, leadership training is given to all the group members.

Skill Training

Each disabled has different potentials and skills, often hidden in them. They have to prove their mettle in their own way, if proper training is given to them. They all have training to put their skills in the right way, so that they become independent in their lives. Suitable trainings to the disabled are computer application, tailoring, processing of fish, soap making, pickles making etc. Marketing can be done through Grama Vasantham (GV). If many GV members buy them for their use, there is no need for other consumers as there were 6,190 members (now it has been taken over by the government and most of the beneficiaries became independent). They can also create links with other organizations, which are part of AID India's network.

Training on manufacturing aids and appliances

If a small group of people gets training on the manufacturing of aids and appliances for the disabled community, it is then useful for the whole community. It is a continuous process. A group can be trained for manufacturing the appliances.

Physiotherapy and medical camp, exposure, and outcomes of the project

Physiotherapy and medical camps for the disabled people

A physiotherapist has to give proper exercises, so that many disabled people will be able to move. The parents have to be trained to handle the PWDs and get training to give physiotherapy to their disabled member in the family at their level.

A camp will be conducted in a center, where possible medical assistance could be given to them. They could get their certificates there, to obtain the identity cards they need to assert their rights (as their prerogatives can only be recognized after many administrative procedures).

Exposure and women groups

It is good to visit disabled organizations and homes where they live independently with regular income generating activities, including group activities. When they are in groups, they are taken to other disabled concerns to have practical training for replication. Since more women SHG are available in the area, it is also possible for them to have exposure in the local area.

Though the need of forming groups for PWDs is high, the formation of women groups is also important. If the women members are given training in savings, credits and income generating activities, they can become economically strong and the families will sustain with good income. Ultimately, it can help to avoid disability in the community. If the women in the families are aware and economically steady, the whole problem can be solved. It is a preventive measure. Hence the formation of SHGs for the women and training for them is always continuous in the area. Both the SHGs of people with disabilities and women can mingle and cooperate with a healthy link.

The important outcomes of the project

With this project, one can easily say (given that the successful examples of PWD groups who are already AID India's beneficiaries) that disabled people can become more confident and self-reliant with an independent living, so that the disabled community is more recognized. They can benefit from referral services, and proper guidance from qualified persons. They can also have proper education and training, in particular awareness on education, health, treatments and prevention of disability, as well as training in decision taking. Through this, they have more job opportunities, and with their savings and credit activities they have regular income. They also have the opportunity to share their experiences during free discussions, mingle more easily with others (especially other organizations and women SHGs) in the mainstream, and have their rights preserved because they are aware of it. The qualities needed for SHGs can grow in them, and thanks to AID India's network, there is a national and international network, which can also give more awareness to the public on the matter.

Conclusion

In the end, human rights issues are inseparable from development projects. Also, the shape of Indian society has to be considered, with the Indian caste system. Although neutrality in matters of religion is one of the Indian Constitution's principles[27], it is not so obvious at the grassroots level. Indeed, "the notion of separation of religious institutions from the governmental institutions is missing from the Indian secularism (…) in a country where religion, constituent of the social life, is closely imbricated to the politics"[28]. In this context, there is an evident tri-functional division, as explained by Georges Dumézil[29], in the Indian society: the religious called *brahmans*, the warriors *kshatriya*, and at the bottom the shopkeepers *vaishya* and domestics *shudra*. Apart from that, we can find the so-called "untouchable", among which the Dalits, who are outside of that scheme. Hierarchy in the Indian society is therefore based on casteism, which allows the upper castes to maintain their power over the system.

Despite the changes initiated by Mahatma Gandhi for the conditions of the untouchables and women, and for Independence obtained in 1947 (which ended up in the Constitution of 1950 guaranteeing fundamental rights), the system is still extremely rigid and uneasy to change. After independence, the Indian

---

[27] The Constitution of India's 42nd Amendment declared India a "sovereign, socialist, secular democratic republic"

[28] MOLINER Christine, « La crise du sécularisme indien », *La Chronique*, N°251, Octobre 2007, p17

[29] DUMEZIL Georges, *L'idéologie tripartite des Indo-Européens*, Collection Latomus, Bruxelles, 1958, 118 p

system came out to be a mix between the traditional system the people had before, and the one left by the British, with a solid administrative machinery. This could have helped the country's development but proved to be very corrupted, and probably the first thing to be changed[30]. Indian society nowadays swings between its ancient traditions and a new system.

It is extremely important to take all of this into consideration because a rigid system added to an endemic corruption, is what leads to the situation today: an extreme poverty affecting half the population. And traditions make things even more difficult because of the Indian strong belief in karma (that is to say the effects of all deeds which make one responsible for one's own life). This belief leads to a certain fatalism of the neglected populations. Added to their religiousness, it also leads to the submissiveness of the lower castes to the upper ones and to the clergy, sometimes abusing their position and money. As a matter of fact, the feeling of belonging to the same social class doesn't turn into a "class consciousness", which could theoretically lead to a struggle. There is no "class consciousness", and access to the collective resources is only individual (that is to say a system of political clientelism). This is certainly a source of stability in the Indian political behaviors, which rely on objective structures (that is to say non-chosen positions and castes), and at the same time on subjective structures (since these categories are seen as natural).

In short, the people just accept the way things are, they accept passively their poor living conditions to the detriment of the entire society, which could benefit from their skills and hiding potential. As we can see in the villages, they live in the instant, because life is difficult, and human relationships, especially family, remain extremely important (each festival being the occasion to gather). But collective is sometimes a burden, which deeply influences people's lives, especially in terms of marriage, which are most of the time "arranged marriages".

---

[30] SRIVASTAVA Chandrika Prasad, *Corruption – India's enemy within*, New Delhi: Macmillan India, 2001, 240p

Traditions lead to a lot of conditionings, which are very difficult to get rid of. Casteism, arranged marriages with dowry[31] are some of them. Therefore, the influence of the western culture, through the medias and with the globalization system, is also limited. There is only an impact when there is a predisposition to accept certain values, since the traditional culture always remains in the backdrop[32]. Among these traditions, the most critical is the women's condition, despite the recent creation of new instances (the Delhi Commission for Women acting in numerous fields including jurisdictional, the Delhi Legal Services Authority, the Indira Gandhi Priyadarshini Vivah Shagun Yoyana giving a financial aid to the poor for the daughters' marriage and the Labour Welfare Board of the Delhi Government helping ill people and destitute women in Delhi with a special attention for women and children). But with corruption prevailing, poor people, and especially women, cannot win. That is why the microcredit system, which brings the lowest castes, and in particular women, back to the mainstream, constitutes both a social and economic success.

All this considered, I can say that this case study on AID India NGO deeply helps to penetrate at the heart of the Indian society, at the grassroots level. This reinforced me in the idea that going on the grassroots level is essential for anyone who truly wants to understand how things work in the reality. And reality in the fieldwork is not easy. But the changes it leads to are so important that it is enough to fight for, because with "Peace, Force and Joy" we can do anything[33]. That is why I would like to end up with a sentence Mr. S. Peter Raj quoted from Martin Luther King: "If you can't fly, then run. If you can't run, then walk. If you can't walk, then crawl. But whatever you do, keep moving - until you reach the goal."

---

[31] Officially, dowry has been prohibited under the Dowry Prohibition Act, Indian law, enacted on May 1, 1961
[32] HOGGART Richard, *La culture du pauvre*, Paris : Editions de Minuit, 1970, 420 p
[33] AID India's guiding motive

Annex A: Teaching program and examples of the essay

MY TEACHING PROGRAM

Teaching English to Teachers at Maria Grace Rural Middle School (until eighth standard – thirteen year old pupils)

Monday, December 10th

• *Sentences of welcome, present and past tense*

– "This is Christopher"

– "Thanks ... You're welcome"

– "It is/was nice to meet you"

– I am/was glad/pleased to meet you"

• *Tenses*

– present tense and present continuous tense

– past tense and past continuous tense

• *Abbreviations*
– would -> 'd
– will -> 'll
– are -> 're
– does not -> doesn't
Etc.

Tuesday, December 11th

• *List of irregular verbs:*
Each one has to answer for one verb

• *Direct to indirect sentences:*
Each one has to find it by him/herself

• *"Let's invent a story" (French game)*
I give one word, each one gives a sentence, and it will make a story. At the same time, we are learning connecting words, and useful things to make proper sentences. Words were "tree" (proposed by me, which became "coconut tree"), and "elephant" (proposed by them).

Wednesday, December 12th

• *Making sure they remember and understood the previous lesson*
Every day at the beginning of the course, they will be asked to answer some questions about things we have seen the day before. If they are not able to answer, we will pay special attention to what was not well understood – as is the case today.

• *Writing a short essay*
An essay about "Life" (half a page) will be written in order to see their level of English and to show them what they have to improve.

Thursday, December 13th

-> *Correction of the essay*

Through active participation, the teachers will try to correct themselves their essays after showing the mistakes in syntax, grammar, as well as the quality of the language to improve with proper words.

Friday, December 14th

-> *Practice*

Monday, December 17th

-> *Reminder*

In a sentence, don't forget: Subject + Verb + Complement

Complement can be:

– article + noun (if singular)

– noun (if plural)

– adjective

etc.

• *Spoken English*

Apologizing

Accepting an apology

Wishes and Greetings

Weather

Tuesday, December 18th

• *Reviewing yesterday's lesson*

Components of a sentence

Spoken English

• *Active and Passive voices*

How to make a sentence from the active to the passive voice, with different tenses

• *Synonyms*

List of useful synonyms

Wednesday, December 19th

-> Grammar

Thursday, December 20th

• Antonyms

List of useful antonyms

• Pronouns

What are pronouns and what are they used for

Friday , December 21st

• Reminder

Reviewing the previous lessons for the next exercise

• Texts with holes

Text where they will have to fill the holes with the appropriate answer using what they learned before

Essay

Life

My family is very poor
I have three children and
one male, two female.
First one name precilla
she studies IIIrd std.
Second one ledije she
studies IInd std. last one
Joney he goes to pre
school. My husband is a
Labour. I am a teacher
work in Venkatrayspuram and
II 5td class teacher, my
students are very brilliant.

Life

I am Elleena. My father
is farmer. I has two brother
and one sister. My husband
work in dubai. My two
brother work in chennai.
My sister is a teacher.
I married in parapadi at
May 28, 2007.

Annex B: Report about the forum

Forum December 8th, 2007, between the Tamil Nadu Government – a Commercial Bank "Indian Overseas Bank" – MAGRES (Maria Grace Rural Educational Society) / AID India and SHG's leaders

Purpose of the forum

This forum was organized in order to give the 7.1 million rupee loan to the thirty-five groups represented at the meeting (groups coming from the Tirunelvedi district).

This forum was organized by AID India as they provided the money to the groups, so that they are able to come. Indeed, this kind of meeting rarely takes place in the area, as many NGOs are expecting that the members pay the money themselves, and as they don't want to because they prefer to save it.

It is a triangle system. Tamil Nadu's Government will grant to the Bank, which will then choose the right groups who will be the beneficiaries. And since they are senior groups and proved their capacity in repayment (100%), the bank is keener to give loans easily.

There are different kinds of loans:

First, the internal loans from their own savings

Then matching grants given by MAGRES or AID India

Third, the loans from the bank, among which different types of loans are also available (according to the seniority of the group and the amount needed):

- direct loans (around 20,000 rupees)
- loans for revolving funds (about 25,000 rupees)
- direct loans again but bigger (which can be asked many times and may go up to 200,000 rupees depending on their experience)
- loans for economic activities (500,000 rupees and above)

AID India was proud to see that one of its groups got a 550,000 rupee (10,000 euro) loan from the bank, which demonstrates its ability and that they are an effective organisation.

The average of loans given was 11,270 rupees (205 euro).

My speech of empowerment and support (inspired by the speech of the writer P. Coelho) translated in Tamil for the groups by Anthony Raj, MARIA GRACE'S secretary

A Poet called Rûmî said, "Life is just like if a king sent someone to a country to realize a specific mission. This person goes there and realizes hundreds of things – but if she didn't do what she was asked for, it is just like if she did absolutely nothing."

For all women who understood their mission – earn their life, raise and educate their children, and make their family happy

For women who watched the road in front of them, and understood that the road would be long

For women who don't try to minimize the difficulties, but try to overcome them

For women who always keep their door open, their hand at work, and their feet in constant movement

For women who personify the proverb: "behind each successful man, there is a woman"

For all women who are here today:

May they be a great example for all women in India and in the world

And may their example multiply

May they have in front of them many difficult days, so that they can end up their work. That way, the next generation will only find the meaning of injustice and ignorance in dictionaries, and never in a human being's life

May this road be long, because its rhythm is the rhythm of change

And change, the real change, is always very long to accomplish.

Thank you.

Annex C: Passbook (enclosure) and translation of the rules and oath

Rules

1. Among group members we should establish the habits of savings from the meager income avoiding luxuries.

2. By remitting ten rupees anyone can become a member of this scheme.

3. Each member should remit a minimum saving of ten rupees to be credited to her account. It is also good to saving more money.

4. Each week the savings are to be remitted as per the decision taken by the group.

5. If anyone fails to remit savings continuously for four weeks, the name of such member will be deleted from the member list.

6. For reasonable causes anyone can withdraw from the program. They can get back the savings. But ten rupees will be retained in the program towards administrative causes.

7. As per the rules of the program, a member can get loan facility.

8. Member should keep this passbook carefully. If it is lost, it can be bought from the secretary by paying five rupees.

Oath of Members

- Women SHG is our program
- We will work hard for the improvement of this program of AID India
- We are the owner, manager and beneficiary of the program
- Every week we will remit the savings and loan repayment without fail
- We will utilize the loans properly
- We will increase the income and improve the family
- We the Group members and office bearers will act with unity
- We believe whole-heartedly the proverb "Thrift will save family and Savings will save the nation"
- We understand that obtaining a loan is a human right and repaying the loan is our duty

Let children be children

1. Let us stop child labour
2. Let us keep the right to learn
3. It is inhumane to involve the children in labour
4. Children's rights are also human rights
5. Let us retain the rights of children
6. Let us make sure of fundamental education to all children
7. Education is the real wealth of children
8. Let us praise girls' education
9. Let us implement the law of the children properly
10. Today's children are tomorrow's leaders
11. Let us not make the loving child a carrier of burdens
12. Let us make the children be happy

Annex D: Report about the staff meeting

Monthly staff report, December 1st, 2007

Sixteen staff members present (among which four are responsible for the four different main districts, and thus responsible for the others) and AID India's general-secretary S, Peter Raj.

A) Prayer

B) Discussion: each staff member will talk about the activities of the groups she (most of them are women) is supervising

1. Susila
- found special area for children to study
- was asked for children's clothes for Christmas by parents
- was asked for loans by women's groups

2. Usha Rani

- promoted two new SHG (one of fourteen members, the other of eighteen members)
- contacted evening classes for children (because there were no proper facilities for education)
- was asked for clothes for Christmas (idea from me: could contact some organization like EMMAUS in France)
- doesn't have any problem in organizing the meetings with women who are very regular
- twenty-four children were adopted (distance adoption) in that village by SOS Diritti Umani of Italy

3. Asila

- is in charge of twenty-six children, but only twenty-four were adopted
- is having a project to build houses in Kanyakumari Dt, but the government doesn't want to help this tsunami affected area, as it gave money to that village before the disaster
- had special care for children who are now doing well at school
- noticed that a new business of seaweed cultivation to be eaten started (beides the main activity which is related to fishing to sell either fresh or dry fish)

4 Visaya Rani

- faced a problem of child labour (children looking after the porks supposed to be sold)
- noticed that many of these children lived in tents, and not even in houses
- concluded that these children needed special education as they didn't go to school

- settled a tuition center, and children were regularly going there except for four who ran away because they liked watching after porks and playing at the same time better
- is now sending them to school but parents are angry because they lost income
- organized a big meeting with all groups' representatives and animators, Shantha came to talk about education and health, and also Rja Mal, Iyyapan and Christopher who talked about government orders and latest facilities (to raise funds, get lands, etc.)
- promoted two new SHG
- arranged loans for two groups
- added that people were very happy of my personal visit

5. Rajammal

- promoted three groups: one in a very remote village (no bus service at all) and two in another isolated area (where transportation facilities are not very good
- is dealing with the demand of many groups for loans
- is organizing meeting with local commercial banks to get small loans. as AID India can't face the huge demand
- took me in different villages

6. Vigy -> working at AID India's farm

7. Eskaline

- is coming from a coastal village, was herself in a SHG

• faced an issue six months ago concerning a Roman Catholic school: there were not enough teachers in that school because they were asked for bribery to get appointment, thus children were affected

• got seventeen children adopted (it was not possible to find for all), who are now staying in different schools

> • has to check up that everything is okay for them, whether they are going to school or not, but it is a difficult work because they are scattered in four different villages. Previously she got Transfert Admission for the same school (at that time, children were staying with one staff member), but after the request of the parents (according to their location, etc.), they were finally sent to different schools in four different villages.

> • is presently taking care of them but it is complicated (sometimes has to check over the weekends, on Sundays)

8. Uma -> only one installment has been repaid from AID India to the commercial bank, so that it is still possible to ask for other loans to face the demand. But, the problem is the bank manager is a lazy person and thus difficult to convince.

9. Praba

> • is coming from the coastal area, where they lost their houses after the tsunami (became homeless)

> • noticed that a community hall (whose roof is made of coconut leaves) was built by a local organization

> • Houses were built after, by Caritas India and the help of the government, but two kilometres from that area (as a new law says that they have to be at least five hundred metres from the seashore, but no land was available close, and they had to go two kilometres further). The problem is that children have to come there on foot four times a day, to go to school and

come back to their home (as they don't get lunch there). So parents are asking for bicycles for the twenty pupils (but as bicycles are 2000 rupees, it is not feasible).

- was asked for children's dresses for Christmas

10. Banumathi -> new staff member representing some groups

11. Dishni

- is coming from Periathalai village (coastal area)
- is satisfied as children go to tuition centers regularly
- was asked for children's dresses for Christmas

12. Asha

- asked for the sponsorship/distance adoption of thirty-three children, but only eight were adopted which caused a problem between them
- supplied educational material
- got loans for four women's groups from commercial banks (revolving funds)
- was glad for my visit

13. Shantha

- is assisting Jikky (new staff member) to know the villages
- is proposing a free medical camp in Tirunelveli for one day in December (with guidance, treatment and medicine, and the presence of doctors), besides the dispency
- is giving in the villages she goes to, medicine and injections

14. Jikky

- has visited all places now
- is aiming at establishing five groups for PWDs (who are organized already but need last arrangements)

15. Pushparani

- is taking care of small villages in Kanyakumari Dt, indirectly affected by the tsunami (as people were involved in fishing)
- bought land thanks to AID India, to build a school for small children because parents who go to work don't take care of them (project proposal to be written to me)
- was asked for loans by twenty groups
- got 106 children adopted
- was asked for children's clothes for Christmas

16. Dency

- supervising group meetings regularly
- 125 children in Periathalai asked for distance adoption but only fifty-two were
- Many groups are demanding loans: the grown-up groups as well as the new ones are in need of loans (smaller loans for the new SHG)
- The bank manager finally accepted her signature instead of Peter Raj's one
- is concentrating on keeping records, and teaching people what is needed for loans
- took me along with her

Annex E: Disabled group details

	DIFFERENTLY ABLED PERSON SHG								
S.No	Name of the SHG	Name of the Village	Date of Formation	No of Members	Bank A/c Number	Name and Place of Bank	Savings	Name of the Animator	Name of the Representative
1	Elanthalir Diff. Abled Special SHG	Periyathalai	14.11.2003	9	5795	Indian Bank, Padukkapathu	8 500	Ravintheran	Ponesakki
2	Thanrambikkai Diff. Abled Special SHG	Pitchivilai	29.12.2003	8	5808	Indian Bank, Padukkapathu	8 600	Arulrani	A. Jothi
3	Roja Diff. Abled Special SHG	Puthanthanuvai	15.12.2004	6	1700	PACB, Puthandharuvai	7 500	Ummurapina	Chithahina
4	Holy Spirit Diff. Abled Special SHG	Periyathalai	15.12.2004	7	55892	Indian Bank, Padukkapathu	9 500	Suresh	Makapan
5	Therasa Diff.Abled Special SHG 2	Arumuganeri	02.06.2004	9	45213	Canara Bank, Arumuganeri	9 850	Esakki	Rani
6	Elanthentel Diff. Abled Special SHG	Periyathalai	12.01.2005	7	16759	Indian Bank, Padukkapathu	6 600	Ganash	Latha
7	Easwari Diff. Abled Special SHG	Padukkapathu	09.04.2005	8	5757	Indian Bank, Padukkapathu	5 500	Suyampulingam	Saraswathi
8	Indira Diff Abled Special SHG	Nochikulam	30.04.2005	11	7181	PGB, Paikulam	9 800	Antoni Micheal	Savarimuthu
9	Grama Vasantham Diff. Abled Special SHG	Udankudi	20.05.2005	7	25519	Canara Bank, Udankudi	6 750	D. Antoniy Stephen	K. Peter Raj
10	St. Valanar Diff. Abled Special SHG	Pothakalanvilai	24.05.2005	7	12978	Canara Bank, Mudalur	5 950	Antoniy Vilbert	Antoniy Suthagar
11	St. Mariyannai Diff. Abled Special SHG	Pothakalanvilai	24.05.2005	7	12979	Canara Bank, Mudalur	6 500	Manikgaraj	Amalathasan
12	Ambethkar Diff. Abled Special SHG	Rettaikinaru (Kombankulam)	19.07.2005	6	17636	IOB, Satankulam	4 750	Kannaki	Mariya Antony
13	Periyar Diff. Abled Special SHG	Kombankulam	19.07.2005	5	17636	IOB, Satankulam	4 750	Pattukrishan	Santhi
14	Kamarajar Diff. Abled Special SHG	Puthukinaru (Pannamparai)	19.07.2005	6	17634	IOB, Satankulam	5 250		Rani
15	Sakthi Diff. Abled Special SHG	Chettikulam	21.07.2005	6	7255	PGB, Paikulam	6 750	Vijiya Kumar	Muthukumar
16	Annai Therasa Diff. Abled Special SHG	Thiruvaranganeri	21.07.2005	5	7254	PGB, Paikulam	3 500	Rajamani	Doora Kunaseeli
17	Seven Star Diff. Abled Special SHG	Mudalur	01.08.2005	7	13062	Canara Bank, Mudalur	6 450	Gershom	Aksal
18	St. Micheal Diff. Abled SHG	Mudalur	01.08.2005	7	13061	Canara Bank, Mudalur	4 550	Ganadurai	Petchimani
19	Therasal HM Diff. Abled Special SHG	Arumuganeri	02.11.2005	12	16759	Canara Bank, Arumuganeri	10 550	Ramesh	Geetha
20	Gandhi Diff. Abled Special SHG	Nodh Pannamparai	06.11.2005	5	18006	IOB, Satankulam	4 550	Sudalai Muthu	Chinnadurai
21	Annai Theresa Diff. Abled Special SHG	Pothakalanvilai	13.12.2005	7	13023	Canara Bank, Mudalur	6 500	Jebarani	Paulraj
22	Azhagu Diff. Abled Special SHG	Valliammalpuram	20.02.2006	5	18146	IOB, Satankulam	4 500	John	Jeya
23	Sri Vinayaga Diff. Abled Special SHG	Arasoor, Poochikadu	20.03.2006	8	16877	Pandiyan Bank, Thaittarmadam	7 550	Esakipandi	Jeyapalan
24	Nambikkai Diff. Abled Special SHG	Pitchikudieruppu	20.03.2006	10	25467	Indian Bank, Padukkapathu	9 550	Ponsiva	Misiniya
25	Elaya Nila Diff. Abled Special SHG	Periyathalai	22.01.2007	8	56244	Indian Bank, Padukkapathu	7 450	Lusiya	Mariya
26	Kalankarai Vilakkam Diff. Abled Special SHG	Peiyathalai	22.01.2007	12	56246	Indian Bank, Padukkapathu	11 550	Bashil	Venista
27	Nathagi Diff. Abled Special SHG	Puthanthanuvai	16.02.2007	7	85741	PGB Thattarmadam	4 600	Jeyam	Rose
28	Holy Sprit Diff. Abled Special SHG	Periyathalai	21.02.2007	5	56316	Indian Bank, Padukkapathu	4 550	Micheal Magipan	Stanlin
29	Thiru. Kaliyana Matha Diff.Abled Special SHG	Pothakalanvilai	04.03.2007	8	45217	Canara Bank, Muthalur	9 500	Murugan	Laela
30	Five Star Diff. Abled Special SHG	Udankudi	15.03.2007	8	16539	Indian Bank, Kulasegarapattanam	5 500	Gavitha	Seelan
31	Gandhi Diff. Abled Special SHG 1	Kombankulam	20.03.2007	8	45821	IOB, Satankulam	7 650	Kamaraj	Leema
32	Roja Diff. Abled Special SHG	Sokkalinkapuram	25.03.2007	7	15632	Canara Bank Mudalur	5 450	Dencil	Selvam
33	Prize Diff. Abled Special SHG	Nazrath	07.04.2007	9	25361	Canara Bank, Nazareth	5 450	Kumar	Joy
34	Grass Diff. Abled Special SHG	Sankarankudieruppu	12.04.2007	8	52314	IOB, Satankulam	6 500	Navaraj	Pappa
35	Thenrampigai Diff.Abled Special SHG	Periyathalai	20.04.2007	8	63965	Indian Bank, Padukkapathu	7 300	Ponmalar	Ravi
36	Malai Arasar Diff. Abled Special SHG	Kayamoh	21.05.2007	7	72172	Baratha State Bank	1 400	Bapria	Segar
			Total	265			Total	235 050	

89

S.No	Village	U/R	Name	Age	Sex	Religion/ Caste	Qulification/ Income	Nature
1	Adayal	R	Selva Ganesh Varadharajan Palayakoil St Adiyal	20	M	Hindu B.C	Uneducated 11000	Mentally Challenged
2	Alagappapuram	K	Yesuvadivam 4/55 South Street Padukkapathu	63	M	Christian B.C	Uneducated 11000	Leflosy Cuked
3	Alagappapuram	R	Cristober 4/40 Velladurai Padukkapathu	12	M	Christian B.C	Class 1-5 11000	Deaf
4	Alagappapuram	R	Bala Ganesh Kanga Nayaki Alagapuram Padukkapathu	20	M	Hindu Others	Post Graduate 11000	Ortho
5	Alagappapuram	R	Delie Savari Murugna Alagapuram Padukkapathu	17	F	Hindu Others	Class - 6-8 11000	Ortho
6	Alagappapuram	R	Dhilaka Sakthikani Alagapuram Padukkapathu	18	F	Hindu Others	Class 9-10 11000	Ortho
7	Alagappapuram	R	Jeyaraja Gurusamy Alagapuram Padukkapathu	58	M	Hindu B.C	Class 1-5 11000	Ortho
8	Alagappapuram	R	Janakiraman Thangaperumal Alagapuram Padukkapathu	40	M	Hindu B.C	Class 1-5 11000	Oktmo
9	Alagappapuram	R	Sakthikani Iliyapeumal Alagapuram Padukkapathu	58	F	Hindu B.C	Class 1-5 11000	Oktmo
10	Alagappapuram	R	Chithira Thomas Middle Street Padukkapathu	12	F	Christian B.C	Class 1-5 11000	Oktmo

List of abbreviations:

AID India: Action In Disabilities India

AVE MARIA: Association of Veteran Employees of Minority Academic
Recognized Institutions of All kind

CNCDH: Commission Nationale Consultative des Droits de l'Homme

FIDH: Fédération Internationale des Droits de l'Homme

GV: Grama Vasantham (microcredit program)

IEP: Institut d'Etudes Politiques

MR: Mentally Retarded

NGO: Non Governmental Organization

NPO: Non Profit Organization

PWD: People with Disabilities

SHG: Self-Help Group

YAC: Youth Advisory Council

Bibliography:

Books

BUMILLER Elizabeth, May you be the mother of a hundred sons, N.Y: Random House, 1990, 220 p

DUMEZIL Georges, L'idéologie tripartite des Indo-Européens, Collection Latomus, Bruxelles, 1958, 118 p

HOGGART Richard, La culture du pauvre, Paris : Editions de Minuit, 1970, 420 p

SRIVASTAVA Chandrika Prasad, Corruption – India's enemy within, New Delhi: Macmillan India, 2001, 240 p

Article

MOLINER Christine, « La crise du sécularisme indien », La Chronique, N°251, Octobre 2007, p17

Speech

YUNUS Muhammad, Acceptance speech at the award ceremony of the World Food Price, December 1994